D1533192

✫Along Wit's Trail

P7-CFC-511

ALONG WIT'S TRAIL

★ | The Humor and Wisdom
of Ronald Reagan | ★

Edited by L. William Troxler

An Owl Book

Holt, Rinehart and Winston | New York

Copyright © 1983, 1984 by L. William Troxler
All rights reserved, including the right to reproduce
this book or portions thereof in any form.
Published by Holt, Rinehart and Winston,
383 Madison Avenue, New York, New York 10017.
Published simultaneously in Canada by Holt, Rinehart
and Winston of Canada, Limited.

Library of Congress Cataloging in Publication Data
Reagan, Ronald.
    Along wit's trail.
    "An Owl book."
    1. Reagan, Ronald—Quotations.   2. Reagan, Ronald—
Anecdotes.   I. Troxler, L. William.   II. Title.
E838.5.R432 1984   973.927'092'4   84-3798
ISBN: 0-03-072019-2
First Owl Book Edition—1984

Printed in the United States of America
10 9 8 7 6 5 4 3 2 1

ISBN 0-03-072019-2

With thanks to Ronald and Nancy Reagan
With appreciation to the President's dedicated supporters
And with love to Mom and Dad

☆ Contents

Foreword   ix

1 ☆
"Once upon a Time in Politics . . ."   1

2 ☆
"Aim Straight and Shoot One-Liners"   24

3 ☆
"That Reminds Me of the One About . . ."   37

4 ☆
"It Takes All Kinds of Jelly Beans"   61

5 ☆
"Well, Thank You, Thank You Very Much"   76

6 ☆
"Remember the Code of the West"   84

7 ☆
"Sincerely Yours, America"   102

★ Foreword

The funniest since Lincoln. The wittiest since Kennedy. The Great Communicator. Here, finally, is a carefully culled collection of the humorous and wise remarks of our nation's fortieth president, Ronald Reagan.

Some of it is hilarious, some isn't supposed to be. All of it is lively reading. Browsing through these pages, you'll come to understand and appreciate how Ronald Reagan manages to endear himself to his friends and confound his opponents. Here, then, are some clues to his success.

This is a collection of all-American anecdotes and actor's axioms, camp-fire corollaries and homespun homilies, sage stories and statesman's speeches, western yarns and Yankee witticisms.

It is a conservative's companion, a liberal's nightmare, and the only published collection of President Reagan's humor and wisdom.

If, as Emerson said, "language is the archives of history," then Ronald Reagan's talents should be long preserved. With his wisdom, he inspires and informs. With his humor, he entertains and comforts. At once he combines both to steer the ship of state.

So what makes Ronald Reagan's humor so effective? How

does one man so brilliantly fuse wit, intellect, warmth, and political savvy? Some answers lie in his unique personality traits but also in that stuff we call "humor."

Some say humor is the most mature form of defense against tension, anger, and hostility. They say it is a highly developed way to bandage and heal the wounds of political war. Humor used effectively in tense moments—such as fighting liberals in Congress for budget cuts—decreases conflict to a level that allows the President and his political adversaries to focus on unresolved issues. A well-timed joke opens the most sensitive issues for discussion. A carefully planned yet apparently spontaneous quip eases a possibly offensive remark, or deflects a political potshot, while thoroughly engaging the opponent.

These subtle techniques have time and again enabled Ronald Reagan to wear down his opposition, while crystalizing his own political position.

Ronald Reagan frequently aims his humor at himself, dissolving the oft-portrayed image of him as a distant chairman-of-the-board-type leader and showing that he shares the personal hopes and fears of his audience.

The personality traits that make President Reagan so effective in his use of humor are self-evident to his longtime admirers. His behavior is remarkable in its diversity. He has succeeded in many roles—actor, rancher, loving husband and father, political showman, strategic planner, and jolly grandfather.

Life has been a good stage for him. No matter what the situation, his manner is consistently relaxed and apparently spontaneous. His verbal delivery is remarkably smooth, natural, and directed at the individual. Even when he is reading a prepared speech text, his presentation is authentic, sincere, and commands attention.

He conveys an emotional presence that is warm and sanguine. His Irish heritage is pronounced: an engaging smile, affection for the humorous yarn, and genuine concern for those around him.

At the same time his attitudes and actions are appropriate to the presidency, reflecting a deeply felt desire to lead America.

While offering a leader's vision, his intellect still focuses on the daily "crises" that every occupant of the Oval Office must face alone. Recall the attempt on his life, the PATCO strike, the assassination of his friend Anwar Sadat, the brutal attacks on the Korean jetliner and the marine camp in Lebanon, and the rescue mission in Grenada. In each situation he was decisive, firm in his decisions, and ever resolute in his convictions.

A look at Ronald Reagan's relaxed manner, Irish charm, and pragmatic intellect, then, helps to show why he has survived and succeeded politically and will likely continue to achieve through the years.

This collection has a second purpose, and that is to aid the "once in a blue moon" toastmaster who is suddenly called on to lead a discussion, host a conference, or shine in a seminar setting. Employing Ronald Reagan's material will not a sterling speaker make, but his humor and wisdom can only help to lighten and enliven the remarks, arouse the interest of an audience, and win its attention.

For the reader who is serious about joking around, the chapters are loosely organized so that form more or less follows function.

Chapter 1 introduces Ronald Reagan's favorite stories and old yarns. Here are some pearls from his days as a college student, later as governor of California, en route to the Executive Mansion and, of course, as the current tenant in the people's house. Blended in are stories he uses to help audiences understand political esoterica, to win over opponents, or simply to establish rapport with the particular group to whom he is speaking.

Chapter 2 is loaded with the one-liners that Ronald Reagan

is famous for—the quick-fire, sure-fire antidotes to the worries and woes of Washington.

Chapter 3 has just good old-fashioned jokes; the two farmers . . . the farmer and the lawyer. . . . Sorry, he doesn't tell farmer's daughter jokes. Indeed, this collection is for those who are dismayed with the current popularity of "disgusting jokes" books.

Chapter 4 contains an assortment of quips, wry turns of phrase, and typically Reaganesque ways of looking at our world. The title, "It Takes All Kinds of Jelly Beans," derives from a cabinet meeting a few years back. The President was walking around the table with the now famous jar of jelly beans and offering them to everybody, while musing, "You can tell a lot about a man by whether he picks out a certain color or reaches in and grabs a handful."

Chapter 5 is brief and to the point. It shows various ways of "warming up" the audience when starting a speech.

Chapter 6 is mostly in a serious vein, giving thoughtful advice always mixed with humor to soften the didactic edge.

Chapter 7 wraps up with Ronald Reagan sharing his selections from the presidential mailbag. Even with a busy schedule, he always finds time to read and answer some of the thousands of letters he receives each week.

☆

If in this first effort to show the full range of Ronald Reagan's public remarks there are notable omissions, they are not intentional. Over the years in his remarkable career he has said and done a great deal. Indeed, long before John Kennedy was being credited for transforming the presidency into boffo TV, Ronald Reagan was in Hollywood sparkling before the camera lens. A complete survey of his comments might grace a library table, but this is more of a vest-pocket companion, with emphasis on some of the President's favorites.

Along Wit's Trail reminisces and remembers, reflects and records the goings-on of the past few years. In these pages are stories about Jimmy Stewart and Bob Hope, James Watt and Jesse Helms, the Washington Redskins and *Penthouse*, Knute Rockne and Jimmy Durante.

Occasionally, and when necessary, the material is introduced, explaining to whom, about what, and why he was speaking.

And as with most humor, much is begged, some is borrowed, and a little stolen. After all, some jokes are immortal, handed down through the ages, polished a little, and delivered over and over again.

Bear in mind that these statements are edited just lightly for publication. The words appear more or less as originally spoken, and since half the effect of a good story or a thoughtful moral is in the telling—you know, "you had to be there"—a certain amount is lost in translation to the printed page. So when browsing through, read as if you were hearing and laugh as if you were there with him.

Cheerful reading!

L. William Troxler
January 1984

✯ Along Wit's Trail

1 ★ "Once upon a Time in Politics . . ."

I had to work hard to put myself through school. But it wasn't all that bad. One of the better jobs I had at Eureka College was washing dishes in the girl's dormitory.

I can't resist doing a little reminiscing and telling a story that has to do with American football and soccer. It was years ago, in the days of a coach named Knute Rockne at Notre Dame—the great and famous football school of the time.

He would have upward of one hundred men turn out at the beginning of the season, and then he had to cut the squad. He figured out an easy way to cut the squad.

On the first day he divided them up into two groups, one here and one there. And he went out with a soccer ball and put it down and made a little speech: "I want that group to try to kick the ball across the goal line, and this group, you try to stop them and kick it across that goal line."

He said, "Of course, you know, you may have to do a little shin-kicking at the same time. But as I say, football is a game of courage."

He looked down, and the soccer ball was gone. He said, "All right, come on, who took the soccer ball?" And the littlest guy there said, "Never mind the ball, Rock, when do we start kicking?"

☆

In the exuberance of youth I was not as understanding of the folks trying to pay the bills and meet the budget as I am now.

I ended up participating as a freshman in the first student protest in the history of my college.

But before you decide you're face-to-face with a student radical, let me say that even now, in hindsight, I believe our cause was just. And we didn't break a single window, and we had no picket lines, and we didn't carry any placards or signs.

☆

Back at Eureka College when I was playing football, one night we were having a chalk talk with the coach.

I had never gone into a game in my life that I hadn't said a prayer, but I never would have said so to the guys around me. I thought I was probably the only one in the world who ever did that. Somehow the subject came up about prayer. I sat there and listened. Every fellow in that room, it developed, did the same thing.

Now, I know what I'd figured out for myself should be a prayer. You can't ask to win because the Lord's got to be on everyone's side, but there are things you can ask. And one by one, every one of us, on our own and never having admitted it before, had come up with the same idea.

You can't ask to win, but you can ask that He help you to do your best and, having done your best, you'll have no regrets no matter how it turns out, and you will be content with the outcome. Just may the best one win.

☆

Some years later, while I was governor—during those riotous days when universities were in flames—if I went to a campus, I'd start a riot.

Finally some student leaders from the University of California campus demanded to see me as governor. Well, they came to see me. Some of them were barefoot—the custom of the day in those riotous times—and they all sat around, and one of them was the spokesman. He said, "Governor, it's impossible for you to understand our generation."

Well, I tried to pass it off. I said, "We know more about being young than we do about being old." He said, "No, I'm serious. You can't understand your own sons and daughters."

He continued, "You didn't grow up in an age of instant electronics, of jet travel, of space travel, and of journeys to the moon. You didn't have . . . " And he went on and on—cybernetics and all the things that we didn't have.

Well, he talked just long enough so that I had time to think, and I said, "You're absolutely right. Our generation didn't have those things when we were your age. We invented them."

☆

Mr. Reagan, talking to the National Association of Student Councils about government paperwork and bureaucracy:

3

I know of a teacher who realized one day that the form he kept getting, kept filling out, and kept sending in asked some of the same questions over and over again, such as what was the size of his classroom.

He got curious as to whether anybody in Washington ever read those reports, so each time he filled out the same old form, he increased the size of his classroom until he got it up to the size of the Colosseum. But there was no protest from Washington.

Then he went the other way. He started reducing it so that his classroom was smaller than a steamer trunk, and still there was no word from Washington. That's when he decided, "Why fill them out? No one's reading them."

This is the type of excess bureaucracy we can do without.

I have a warm spot for school principals. I was in the principal's office once in Dixon High School, and I wasn't in there just to pass the time of day. Well, at one point he said to me, "You know, I don't care what you think of me now, I'm only interested in what you think of me fifteen years from now."

Mr. Reagan, back in a grammar school classroom:
I thought maybe you asked me here to a remedial English class because you heard my speeches.

Mr. Reagan, on living in the White House:
When I was a kid my father worked in a store; we lived above the store. It's no different from the White House, except that now I go to work in an elevator.

The third grade teacher was trying to impress on her students that winter had come along, and she was trying to tell

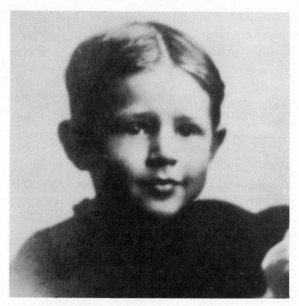

Ronald Reagan as a child

them how to avoid colds. She told a very heartrending tale about her little brother.

As the story went, her little brother was a fun-loving boy, and he went out with his sled, stayed out too long, caught cold, then pneumonia, and three days later he was dead.

When she finished with the tale, there was silence in the room. She thought she had really gotten through to them when a voice in the back said, "Where's his sled?"

Every time I talk about intelligence and wisdom, I think of the old legend of the three wise men on the island that was threatened with being flooded by a hurricane.

One of them decided that in the limited time left he would do all the things he had never been able to do in his life.

The second one devoted himself to further study.

The third one was a good pattern for everyone—he retreated with his closest advisers to the highest point on the island and set out to determine whether they could live under water.

☆

Many years ago, in the days of austerity in England just after the labor government had gotten in, I arrived for the royal command performance at the Savoy Hotel.

I went down to the dining room. There was rationing, and you couldn't get food such as we have today; but then on the menu I saw pheasant. And I thought, well, you can't go wrong if you order pheasant, so I ordered it.

But I didn't know about their custom of serving game birds. Well, the waiter came out and with a flourish removed the lid, and I was looking at a bird that was looking back at me: The head and the ruff were on, the eyes were open, and the big yellow legs were attached to him. It did kind of curb my appetite a little.

The following day another American arrived and ordered the pheasant. I watched, without saying a word, the same flourish from the waiter, and there was the bird, staring back.

As the waiter started away, the American grabbed him by the coattail, saying, "Bring me liniment, and I'll have the bird flying again in fifteen minutes."

☆

Some years ago, when I was governor, I spoke in Mexico City. After I had finished, I sat down to rather unenthusiastic applause, and I was a little embarrassed.

The speaker who followed me spoke in Spanish—which I didn't understand—and he was being applauded about every paragraph.

To hide my embarrassment, I started clapping before everyone else and longer than anyone else until our ambassador leaned over and said, "I wouldn't do that if I were you; he's interpreting your speech."

☆

Back when I was governor, at Thanksgiving time the turkey growers brought in a cooked turkey for me to carve, and we'd have lunch right there with the staff in the office.

But I had to carve it for all those ladies and gentlemen of the press with their cameras on me.

I remember one day I was carving, and I thought they hadn't cooked it very well because there was quite a bit of blood appearing, which didn't look very appetizing.

I found out I'd cut my thumb. Sort of spoiled lunch.

I can remember when there weren't so many Republicans in California, when not too long ago Republicans seemed as plentiful as spring water in Death Valley.

And I speak with authority because I spent a good chunk of my life on that piece of real estate.

Then there was the Mississippi Republican, the first to try for a seat in this old southern district. He dropped in on a farm there, and he told the farmer he was the Republican candidate for Congress in the district.

The farmer's eyes popped open, his jaw dropped, and he said, "Wait right here just a minute." He went running across the barnyard yelling, "Ma, Ma." She came out, and back the two came hand in hand. They stood in front of him and said, "We've never seen a Republican before. Would you make a speech?"

Well, he looked around for some sort of platform. The only thing he could see there was a pile of that stuff that it took the late Bess Truman thirty-five years to get Harry to call fertilizer. Anyway, he climbed up on it and made his speech, and they stuck with him.

When he stepped down, they said it was the first time they had ever heard a Republican speech. He said, "Well, that's all right. That's the first time I've ever given a Republican speech from a Democratic platform."

☆

Mr. Reagan was chatting with the National Council of Negro Women when he recalled an old friend with whom he had played football in college—his name was Franklin Burghardt:

In those days not very many of us got to college, and if you did, it was because you could play football or something, which is how I got there.

Anyway, Burky was black, and he meant a lot to us, his teammates. We were playing a game one day, down 14 to 0, with only two minutes remaining in the half.

The other team, which wasn't blessed with someone like Burky, began to pick on him, which was common for the time.

To give you an indication of what we all thought of Burky, we ended the half 14 to 14 and ended the game 43 to 14—he was quite a man.

☆

And then there was Lincoln. As a young lawyer he once had to plead two cases in the same day before the same judge. Both involved the same principle of law. But in one Lincoln appeared for the defendant and in the other for the plaintiff.

Now, you can see how this makes anything above a 50 percent success rate very difficult.

In the morning Lincoln made an eloquent plea and won his case. Later he took the opposite side and was arguing just as earnestly.

Puzzled, the judge asked why the change of attitude. "Your Honor," said Honest Abe, "I may have been wrong in the morning . . . but I know I'm right now."

☆

I have a story, and I hope Jimmy Stewart won't object to my repeating it.

He would introduce me at various banquets along the cam-

paign trail, and every time the emcee introduced him, he would talk about his great stardom in pictures.

Each time I got up, I would apologize to the emcee for correcting him and add about Jimmy's war record—that he not only flew the Hamburg run, but that he was a major general in the Air Corps Reserve.

One time, after several of these situations, the master of ceremonies did refer to Jimmy's military record and then said, "Brigadier General Jimmy Stewart." So when I got up, I apologized to the emcee once again and said, "It's Major General Jimmy Stewart."

That night when we got back to the hotel, Jimmy said, "Ron, that fellow was right—it is brigadier general. I just never corrected you before because it sounded so good."

☆

Mr. Reagan, speaking to the building trades, talked about his first summer job:

I was fourteen years old, working for an outfit remodeling homes for sale.

Before the summer ended I'd laid hardwood floors, shingled roofs, painted ceilings, and dug foundations.

There wasn't a very clear distinction in those days between craft lines in a small town. There also weren't any bulldozers or skip loaders in those days, so the grading was pretty much pick and shovel.

I remember one hot morning I'd been swinging a pick for about four hours. I heard the noon whistle blow. I had been waiting for that sound. I had the pick up over my shoulder ready for the next blow, and when I heard the whistle, I just let go, walked out from underneath it, and let it fall behind me.

I heard a loud scream and then some very strong profane language. I turned around, and the boss was standing right behind me. That pick was imbedded in the ground right between his feet. Two inches either way, and I'd have nailed him.

10

I remembered the incident when I heard the screams about our budget cuts.

☆

A city had decided it was going to raise its traffic signs. They were five feet high, and they were going to raise them to seven.

The federal government stepped in and volunteered with a program to do it—they came in and lowered the streets two feet.

☆

We cannot go back to the glory days of big, never-mind-the-cost government. The best view of that kind of government is in a rearview mirror as we leave it behind.

And we can no longer listen to those who say: "If it's commerce, regulate it; if it's income, tax it; if it's a budget, bust it."

Given their way, they'd make everything that isn't prohibited, compulsory.

A better rule is, "If it ain't broke, don't fix it."

☆

Mr. Reagan was speaking to a tenth anniversary gathering of the organization Executive Women in Government:

There was an accident one day; the victim was lying there, and bystanders had gathered around.

A woman was bending over him trying to help. A man came elbowing his way through the bystanders, shoved the woman aside, and said, "Let me at him. I have first-aid training."

She stepped aside, and he knelt down and started doing the prescribed things in his training. At one point she tapped him on the shoulder and said, "When you get to the part about calling the doctor, I'm right here."

☆

I have an old horror story about government regulations run amok.

There was this fellow in government who sat at his desk, and documents came to his desk, then he marked them for forwarding to the proper destination, initialed them, and passed them on.

One day a classified document came to his desk. Since it had come there, he read it, decided where it should go, initialed it, and passed it on.

A day later it came back to him with an attached memo that said, "You weren't supposed to see this. Erase your initials and initial the erasure."

☆

Mr. Reagan was asked by a high-school student to tell some old stories about the White House:

It used to be that the White House was also the offices of the president's staff and cabinet. Well, old Teddy Roosevelt had six children, and one day his wife told him to get all those employees out or she couldn't raise the six children.

And that's when they built the Oval Office.

☆

Mr. Reagan was praising a leader of the International Longshoremen's Association, and he was joking about what it is like to tangle with the leader:

It might be like those two fellows that were sawing on a tree limb, and one of them fell off. There was a wildcat down below, and there were sounds of a struggle coming up. The one on the limb called down and said, "Hold on." Well, the guy below said, "Hold on? Come down and tell me how to let him go."

☆

Back in America's early days, our people began visiting the lands of their forefathers. American tourists then were rather brash, unsophisticated by European standards, but blessed with the spirit of independence and pride.

The President with his original cabinet

One such tourist, an elderly, small-town gentleman, and his wife were there in Europe listening to a tour guide go on about the wonders of the volcano, Mount Aetna. He spoke of the great heat that it generated, the power, the boiling lava, and all its splendor.

Finally the old boy had had enough. He turned to his wife and said, "We've got a volunteer fire department at home that would put that thing out in fifteen minutes."

Mr. Reagan was illustrating why he opposes the "exclusionary rule" in criminal enforcement:

A few years ago two narcotics agents in San Bernadino,

13

California, had enough evidence to get a warrant to search a home—a couple living there was believed to be peddling heroin.

They searched the home, and they didn't find the heroin. But as they were leaving, one of them, on a hunch, went back to the baby's crib. There was a baby. He took its diapers off, and there was the heroin, stashed inside the diapers.

Well, they went to court. And you know, the judge threw the case out of court on the basis that the baby's constitutional rights had been violated—for taking the diapers off without its permission.

☆

A Democratic congressman from the South was visiting his district. A constituent asked him where he stood on our economic recovery program—particularly the tax cut.

Well, the Democratic congressman, who happens to be a strong leader in support of our program, replied at some length with a discussion of the technical points involved, but he also mentioned a few reservations he had on certain points.

The constituent, a farmer, listened politely until he'd finished, and then he said, "Don't give me an essay. What I want to know is are you for 'im or agin 'im?"

☆

Mr. Reagan, speaking to American troops at Camp Liberty Bell in Korea:

Somebody asked me if I'd be safe up here so close to North Korean troops, and I said, "I'll be with the Second Infantry Division."

Back in World War II days a young draftee was complaining about some of the methods of the army and the way the army did things. So he asked a Regular Army sergeant about it. The sergeant said, "Son, look, if you were in charge of a brand new country and you finally got a division created, what would you call it?"

The kid said, "Well, I guess I'd call it the First Division."

The sergeant said, "Well, in the United States they call the first one the Second Division, and when you understand that, you'll understand everything about the army."

☆

Mr. Reagan was speaking to the Associated General Contractors of America about government red tape:
A fellow in my neighborhood not long ago was building his own home. He got so fed up finally with all the government paperwork that he pasted all the pages together, strung them up on two poles, and had a strip of paper 250 feet long.

☆

Mr. Reagan, on the eve of St. Patrick's Day, wishing for a miracle in his best Irish accent:
There was a little tad who was in court in New York, bandaged from his toes to his chin, suing for $4 million as the result of an accident, and he won the suit. The lawyers for the insurance company came over to him and said, "You're never going to enjoy a penny of this. We're going to follow you twenty-four hours a day. We know you're faking, and the first time you move, we'll have you."

He said, "Will you now? Well, let me tell you what's going to happen to me. They're coming in here with a stretcher, they're taking me out, and downstairs they're putting me in an ambulance. They're driving me straight to Kennedy Airport, and they're putting me on the airplane on that stretcher. We're flying direct to Paris, France, and there, they're taking me on the stretcher off the plane, putting me in another ambulance. That ambulance is going directly to the shrine of Lourdes, and there you're going to see the damndest miracle you ever saw." ☆

Mr. Reagan, the next day with the Irish ambassador, still caught up with an infectious brogue:
As I've said before, I grew up knowing very little about my

family tree. I would meet other people of the name Reagan or Regan—we're all of the same clan—but never understand the spelling difference.

Well, I was joking with Treasury Secretary Donald Regan; I told him that his branch of the family just couldn't handle that many letters. It was then that he explained to me that the "Regan" clan were the professional people and the educators, and only the common laborers called it "Reagan."

So, meet a common laborer.

I remember when Ezra Taft Benson was secretary of agriculture. He was out in the country and hearing reports from people in the farm areas. At one place there was a fellow who was really giving him a bad time, really complaining.

Well, Ezra turned around, reviewed some notes handed to him by one of his aides, then turned back and said, "Now wait a minute. You didn't have it so bad. You had twenty-six inches of rain this last year."

And the fellow said, "Yes, I remember the night it happened."

☆

I had the pleasure of appearing before a Senate committee once while I was governor. I was challenged because there had been a Republican president in the White House for several months, and they wanted to know why we hadn't corrected everything yet.

I told the Senator about a ranch that Nancy and I had acquired many years ago. It had a barn with eight stalls in which they had kept cattle, and we wanted to keep horses. So I was in there day after day with a pick and shovel lowering the level of those stalls where it had piled up over the years.

And I told this senator that I discovered you cannot undo in weeks or months what it has taken some fifteen years to accumulate.

☆

Mr. Reagan, speaking to Baseball Hall of Famers, waxed nostalgic about his radio broadcast days at station WHO:

We were doing the Cubs games by telegraphic report. There was a fellow on the other side of the window with a little slit underneath, with headphones on, getting dot-and-dash Morse code from the ballpark and typing it out for me. For instance, the paper would come through saying "S1C." Well, you're not going to sell Wheaties yelling "S1C!" So I'd say, "And so-and-so comes out of the windup, here's the pitch, and it's called a strike, breaking over the outside corner."

Well, this one day I saw him start to type, so I began. Dizzy Dean was on the mound, and I started the ball on the way to the plate. Curly, the guy on the telegraph, was shaking his head, and I thought maybe it was a miraculous play or something. But when the slip came through it said, "The wire has gone dead."

Well, I had the ball on the way to the plate, so I figured real quick that we could tell them what happened and then play transcribed music. But in those days there were at least seven or eight other fellows doing the same ballgame, and I didn't want to lose the audience.

I thought to myself: There's one thing that doesn't get in the score book, so I had him foul one off. I looked at Curly, and he just shrugged, so I had him foul another one. And I had him foul one back at third base and described the fight between the two kids who were trying to get the ball. Then I had him foul one that just missed being a home run by a foot and a half.

I set a world record for successive fouls. But now, when I was beginning to sweat, Curly sprang to life, sat up straight, and began typing. The slip came through the window, and I could hardly talk for laughing because it said, "He popped out on the first pitch."   ☆

There's a great deal of discussion about the truth, as if there are degrees of truth.

I remember my first experience with broadcasting the truth as a sports announcer. Using the telegraph, I submit that I told the truth—it was just attractively packaged.

In those days of radio you had a sound-effects man in the studio. He had a wheeled cart, and on it he had every kind of device in the world for the studio dramas, from coconut shells that he beat on his chest to be a galloping horse, to cellophane he could crumple for a fire.

One day we had a play that called for the sound of water falling on a board. Well, during rehearsal the poor fellow tried everything—rice on a drum, dried peas on cardboard—but nothing would give him the sound of water on a board.

Finally, one day he tried water on a board, and you know, it sounded just like water on a board.

☆

I take a lot of ribbing for praising silent Cal Coolidge, but he was a real communicator.

He was having his hair cut once in a one-chair barbershop up in Vermont, and the town doctor came in, sat down, and said, "Cal, did you take the pills I gave you?" Coolidge said nothing for a minute or two, then in his usual articulate style he said, "Nope." A little later the doctor asked, "Well, are you feeling any better?" Another long silence and then he said, "Yup."

Well, his haircut was finished, and he started to leave. The barber hesitantly said, "Aren't you forgetting something?" An embarrassed Coolidge replied, "Oh, yeah, I'm sorry. I forgot to pay you. I was so busy gossiping with the doctor, it slipped my mind."

☆

Mr. Reagan, talking to the National Hockey League All-Star Teams:

Some years back the Carnegie Foundation was investigating what they thought was an overemphasis on sports in American colleges and universities.

Notre Dame's football coach, Knute Rockne, was asked by his fellow coaches to represent them in presenting another side of the story. In one of his appearances before the delegation, an academician said, "Well, Coach Rockne, football is such a violent sport. Why couldn't you put as much emphasis on less violent sports?" Rockne said, "Like what?" And he said, "Hockey."

Knute responded, "Professor, I once suggested hockey to the president of Notre Dame, and he told me that Notre Dame would never back a game that puts a club in the hands of an Irishman."

☆

Mr. Reagan, swearing in the new president of the National Press Club:

One of my favorites, Cal Coolidge, dedicated this building. I'm sure you all remember how he answered an inquisitive lady who said she had a bet that she could get more than three words out of him. He looked at her for a minute and then said, "You lose."

I feel a sense of humility standing here in the same building where silent Cal laid the cornerstone, Harry Truman played the piano, and Richard Nixon ate a hamburger.

What's left for me? The cornerstone is already in place, I can't play the piano, and my food taster is home sick—something he ate, no doubt.

☆

Jerry Carmen, a commonsense, independent businessman from New Hampshire, heads up the General Services Administration for me.

He told journalist Don Lambro about a warehouse with a leaky roof that he went to inspect one Saturday, early in his tenure at GSA. Arriving back at his office, he said, "I asked the people in charge, wasn't that a pretty poor warehouse? And they agreed it was. Well then, I asked them, shouldn't it be closed? And they all said yes. I asked, why don't we? Well, they said, we're going to do a study first. The study was going to cost $500,000. I said, do I have the power to close it? They said that I did. And I did."

Mr. Reagan, speaking to students participating in International Youth Exchange Programs:

Just after World War II, I was in England. One weekend I went out to the countryside to see one of the fabulous ancient pubs. The driver apologized when he stopped at one that was only four hundred years old—he hadn't been able to find a really old one.

20

Well, we went in; it was a mom-and-pop operation—you know, the old gentleman at the bar and a matronly woman. She came in and took our order. After hearing us for a few seconds, she said, "You're Americans, aren't you?" I allowed as how we were. She said, "Oh, there were a lot of your chaps stationed down the road during the war. They used to come in and hold songfests. They called me Mom, and they called the old boy Pop."

She continued on, "It was Christmas Eve"—and by this time she's not looking at us anymore; she's kind of looking off into the distance, and her eyes are beginning to fill up. "It was Christmas Eve, and we were here all alone. The door opened, and in they came. And they had presents, Christmas presents for me and Pop."

By this time the tears were rolling down her cheeks. She managed: "Big strappin' lads, they was, from a place called Ioway."

☆

The first time I traveled in France, it was with an English couple, and though they lived just twenty miles away across the Channel, they didn't know one word of French.

We were coming to a town for lunch, and I tried to remember some French from high school. I mentally figured out how to ask about lunch—it was *gendarme*. Well, I rolled down the window of the car and said, *"Pardon, monsieur, j'ai grand faim. Où est le meilleur café?"* And he told me where the best café was.

As we started on, my friend who was driving said, "What did he say?" And I said, "I haven't the slightest idea. I memorized the questions, never the answers."

☆

I have a true story; it involves a fellow Californian, Danny Villanueva, who used to place-kick for the Rams and then later became a sports announcer.

Danny was having dinner one night at the home of a young

ball player with the Dodgers. He and the ball player were talking sports, and his wife was bustling about getting dinner ready. The baby started to cry, and she shouted over her shoulder, "Change the baby."

Being a young fellow and kind of inexperienced, he was embarrassed in front of Danny, and he said, "What do you mean, change the baby? That's not my line of work, I'm a ball player."

She turned around, put her hands on her hips, and communicated. She said, "Look, buster, you lay the diaper out like a diamond, you put second base on home plate, put the baby's bottom on the pitcher's mound, hook up first and third, slide home underneath. And if it starts to rain, the game ain't called; you start all over again."

I hope Margaret Thatcher won't mind my telling this story.

I knew our first get-together was going to be around the dinner table at the White House, so I was all set. When we sat down I was going to say, "Margaret, if one of your predecessors had been a little more clever, you'd be hosting this gathering."

I underestimated her because as we sat down I said, "Margaret, if one of your predecessors had been a little more clever—" She said, "I know, I would have been hosting this gathering."

Mr. Reagan is fond of telling an old World War II story about heroism in the skies over Nazi-occupied Europe. In December 1983, members of the media tried to prove the story untrue. A month later, after rummaging through files and more files, war historians found a story very similar to Mr. Reagan's. Even if they had not, God forbid, this story shows how a leader can use a striking visual metaphor to excite a nation to believe in itself:

One of our B-17s was coming back across the Channel from a raid over Europe badly shot up by antiaircraft; the ball turret on the belly of the plane had taken a hit. The young ball-turret gunner was wounded, and they couldn't get him out of the turret while in flight.

But over the Channel the plane began to lose altitude, and the commander had to order "bail out." As the men started to leave the plane, the boy saw he was going down with the plane, and he cried out in terror. The last man to leave the plane saw the commander sit down on the floor. He took the boy's hand and said, "Never mind, son. We'll ride it down together."

Congressional Medal of Honor posthumously awarded.

2 "Aim Straight and Shoot One-Liners"

You know, there are only two places where communism
works: in heaven, where they don't need it, and in hell,
where they've already got it.

☆

Where else but in Washington could they call the department that's in charge of everything outside and out-of-doors
the Department of the Interior.

We can make America stronger, not just economically and militarily, but also morally and spiritually. We can make our beloved country the source of all the dreams and the opportunities that she was—
(At this point, a balloon popped in the arena, sounding like a gunshot.)
Missed me . . .

I can define middle age—it's when you're faced with two temptations, and you choose the one that'll get you home by nine o'clock.

I had an uncle who was a Democrat in Chicago. He received a silver cup from the party for voting in fourteen straight elections—he'd been dead for fifteen of them.

I've been trying to meet the Democratic members of Congress halfway, and the halfway house I found is Tip O'Neill's office.

I got an unsigned valentine, and I'm sure it was from Fritz Mondale. The heart on it was bleeding.

There are two ways of doing things: the right way, and the way they do it in Washington.

☆

America didn't run up a trillion-dollar debt because government didn't tax enough; we're straddled with a trillion-dollar debt because government spends too much.

☆

That bureaucratic monster who would slay private enterprise is learning a new command, and it's called "Heel."

☆

We are a nation that has a government, not the other way around.

☆

Until someone can prove the unborn child is not a life, shouldn't we give it the benefit of the doubt and assume it is?

☆

We didn't go to Washington with more snake-oil remedies and quick fixes; we don't suffer from paralysis by analysis.

☆

At my age I didn't go to Washington to play politics as usual.

☆

The picture of fear and despair that they paint on the network evening blues—that's a picture of America where she was, not where she's going.

☆

When you mention common sense in Washington, you cause traumatic shock.

☆

You spell our progress against inflation and interest rates R-E-L-I-E-F.

☆

Probably the most accurate description of the American Revolution was given to me by an Englishman who said they understood it was just an argument between two groups of Englishmen.

☆

Accepting a government grant with its accompanying rules

is like marrying a girl and finding out her entire family is moving in with you before the honeymoon.

☆

Competition is good.

☆

Imagine having two Tip O'Neills.

☆

The Washington establishment believes that the only good dollar is the one taken from a taxpayer's pocket.

☆

In Washington people don't realize that you can't drink yourself sober or spend yourself rich; that you can't prime the pump without pumping the prime.

☆

If we're to renew America, we must stop trying to homogenize it.

☆

Mr. Reagan was speaking to a large audience, and a few demonstrators in the back of the room were shouting, trying to interrupt him. The President had ignored them for a bit, and then:
You know, I spoke here in 1975, and there wasn't an echo.

☆

I feel a great affinity for James Madison. I'm told that his worry over the size of the national debt drove him to distraction. I can sympathize; the debt was not of his making either.

☆

We've got to get government off your backs and out of your pockets.

☆

When we came to Washington, we made quite a stir. Everybody found out that we were going to do just what we said we were going to do.

☆

Mr. Reagan, leaving the White House for his annual physical checkup, was asked by reporters how he was feeling:
Hungry.

☆

In Washington the economists have a Phi Beta Kappa key at one end of the watch chain and no watch at the other.

☆

There was a Democrat during the campaign who told a large group, "Don't worry, I've seen Ronald Reagan, and he looks like a million . . ."
He was talking about my age.

☆

Washington is the only city where sound travels faster than light.

☆

If I could paraphrase Will Rogers's line about never having met a man he didn't like, it seems some in government have never met a tax they didn't hike.

☆

Enough of the policies of tax and tax, spend and spend, elect and elect.

☆

Mr. Reagan, to the big spenders in Congress:
Why is it inflationary for citizens to spend their money the way they want to and not inflationary when government takes that money and spends it the way government wants to?

☆

To those who say that we can't cut spending, lower tax rates, reduce inflation and, yes, rebuild the defenses we need in this dangerous world, I have a six-word answer: Yes we can, yes we must!

☆

I know you've been reading a lot about what's going on here in Washington. Some of it is true.

☆

We've been trying to follow the advice of Mark Twain, which was, "Do what's right and you'll please some of the people and astound the rest."

☆

There's an old saying: In levying taxes, as in shearing sheep, it's best to stop when you get to the skin.

☆

Sometimes when a cabinet meeting starts to drag, I wonder what would happen if the jar on the table was filled with jalapeño jelly beans.

☆

We negotiate from strength.

☆

America is the lion's heart of democracy. We have an obligation to give that democracy a voice and even an occasional roar.

☆

Did you hear that the Communists now have a million-dollar lottery for their people? The winners get a dollar a year for a million years.

☆

Well . . .

☆

One of the best signs that our economic program is working is that they don't call it Reaganomics anymore.

Now that we've licked inflation, not only have food prices stopped rising but they've actually declined. For a time there it looked as if it might be cheaper to eat money.

Mr. Reagan, speaking to reporters late in the 1980 campaign:
If not us, then who? If not now, when?

I was going to take up tennis again until I found out you couldn't get the horse on the court.

I don't know of any place where prayer is more needed than in Washington, D.C.

Mr. Reagan was asked by a supporter if he liked being president more than being a movie actor:
Yes, because here I get to write the script too.

☆

I would never accuse our political opponents of ignorance. It's just that there are so many people in Washington who know so many things that aren't true.

☆

Our opponents try to cure the fever by eating the thermometer.

☆

The big spenders in Washington would have been right at home with Oscar Wilde. He's the one who said that he knew of only one way to get rid of temptation: Yield to it.

Mr. Reagan, signing the government Prompt Payment Act, which had been delayed a day:
I would have signed it right away except that the government didn't pay its pen bill on time, so I didn't have anything to write with.

☆

Mr. Reagan, to the admitting staff at George Washington University Hospital on that fateful March day in 1981:
I sure hope you're all Republicans.
To the team of surgeons: If I'd gotten this much attention in Hollywood, I wouldn't have left.
To his First Lady: Guess I should have ducked.
To doctors just thirteen days after the shooting, as they gave their okay for him to go home: I'd already made up my mind on that.
To hospital staffers as he was leaving: I walked in here; I'm going to walk out.
By telephone to the White House press corps at their annual dinner a month later: If I could give you one little bit of advice, when somebody tells you to get in a car quick, do it.

☆

Our loyalty is to the little taxpayers, not the big tax spenders.

☆

Everything we've accomplished has been kept a pretty good secret by the *Washington Post*.

☆

Why are we concerned about El Salvador? For one, it is closer to Texas than Texas is to Massachusetts.
Now, I mean that geographically, not necessarily ideologically.

☆

Mr. Reagan summed up the Soviet military buildup by referring to a newspaper cartoon:
It was Brezhnev speaking to a Russian general, saying, "I liked the arms race better when we were the only ones in it."

☆

Common sense in Washington is about as common as a Fourth of July blizzard in South Carolina.

☆

When we arrived in Washington, we felt a little like Noah must have felt the morning he left the ark to begin all over again.

☆

Our opponents preach like apostles of fairness. Well, maybe they are fair in one way—their policies don't discriminate, they bring misery to everybody.

☆

Washington has a way of being the last to catch on.

☆

Feeding more dollars to government is like feeding a stray pup. It just follows you home and sits on your doorstep asking for more.

☆

Mr. Reagan was asked what advice he would give to a young person going out in the world today:
Vote Republican.

☆

We've made so many advances in my lifetime; for example, I have lived ten years longer than my life expectancy when I was born—a source of annoyance to a great many people.

☆

On the way out here to Montana, I told Air Force One's pilot to fly low over Mount Rushmore—I just wanted to see if they were adding any new faces.

☆

We don't have anything like the Rockies back in Washington. We have one mountain. The big spenders have been working on it for forty years. It's called the national debt.

☆

Mr. Reagan was in attendance at a tribute to Jimmy Stewart:
You know, when Jack Warner, head of Warner Brothers, first heard that I was running for governor of California, he said, "No, no. Jimmy Stewart for governor; Reagan for best friend."

☆

Mr. Reagan was asked by a reporter why extraordinary security measures were being taken to protect the White House from possible terrorist attack. Dump trucks were brought in to block entrances, and ground-to-air missiles had been installed:
I just feel such popularity must be deserved.

☆

The source of our economic problems is finally beginning to dawn on the bafflegabbers and those fancy dudes in Washington. They're finally realizing what Montanans have known for a long time: Government is too big, and it spends too much.

☆

Remember when they were calling what was ailing America a "malaise." And now, former Vice President Malaise is running for president, promising he can do everything just like they did before.

There is no better federal program than an expanding American economy.

☆

I've always thought that Washington didn't have the same problems other cities did to a certain extent because they grabbed hold of the fastest growing industry in America.

☆

What was once a federal helping hand is quickly turning into a mailed fist.

☆

I can't help but agree with the person who likened government to a baby—an alimentary canal with an appetite at one end and no sense of responsibility at the other.

☆

Status quo is Latin for the mess were in.

☆

Evil is powerless if the good are unafraid.

☆

It is my duty as president, and all of our responsibility as citizens, to keep this country strong enough to remain free.

☆

Government's first duty is to protect people, not run their lives.

☆

Some will say our mission is to save free enterprise. Well, I say we must free enterprise to save America.

☆

Many on Capitol Hill are like that gal in the musical *Oklahoma!* who just couldn't say no.

☆

The government is experiencing withdrawal symptoms, and we mustn't feed the habit by injecting more tax dollars into it.

☆

Balancing the budget is a little like protecting your virtue: You just have to learn to say no.

☆

The First Amendment was never meant to expel God from our classrooms.

☆

The federal government has taken too much tax money from the people, too much authority from the states, and too much liberty with the Constitution.

☆

We've moved against waste, fraud, and abuse in government—we've cut back on the federal flood of flicks, flacks, and foldouts.

☆

Entrepreneurs are the forgotten heroes of America.

☆

It's great to be back in California. Right now I really wouldn't rather be in Philadelphia.

☆

America is back!

Our tax system should be made more simple, fair, and rewarding for all the people. Would you believe that even Albert Einstein had to ask the IRS for help on his 1040?

3 ⭐ "That Reminds Me of the One About . . ."

M r. Reagan was addressing a conference of the American Conservative Union. In the room were some of his staunchest supporters, and he wanted them to know that he just couldn't divulge too much information about then current negotiations on the budget:

A farmer and a lawyer got into a pretty bad traffic accident. They both got out of their cars; the farmer took one look at the lawyer, walked back to his car, got a package, and brought it back.

There was a bottle inside, and he said, "Here, you look pretty shook up. I think you ought to take a nip of this. It'll steady your nerves." Well, the lawyer did. And the farmer said, "You still look a little bit pale. How about another?" And the lawyer took another swallow. And under the urging of the farmer, he took another and another and another.

And then, finally, he said he was feeling pretty good and asked the farmer if he didn't think that he ought to have a little nip too. And the farmer said, "Not for me. I'm waiting for the state trooper."

If there's one thing you must possess to be a farmer, it's patience. I know how difficult the past several years have been for farmers—so difficult, in fact, that they should change the lyrics of that old song to read, "How you gonna keep them down on the farm after they've seen the grain prices."

A farmer once won the sweepstakes, thousands and thousands of dollars, and someone asked him what he planned to do with all that money. He said, "I'll just keep on farming till it's all gone."

☆

There have been moments in the past months when trying to get through to the big spenders seemed a little like the Quaker who was milking his cow, and the cow kept kicking the bucket over.

He finally stood up and said, "Thou knowest I cannot beat thee. Thou knowest I cannot even curse thee. But dost thou know I can sell thee to someone who will?"

☆

I remember something that happened a long time ago when teachers could talk about religion in the classroom.

The teacher asked everybody who wanted to go to heaven to raise their hands. All hands instantly shot into the air at once, except one, and she was astounded. She said, "Charlie, you mean you don't want to go to heaven?" He said, "Sure, I want to go to heaven, but not with this bunch."

☆

There's a story about a young fellow from the city who hired out to work on a farm during the harvest season.

The first morning everyone was up well before dawn. The new hired hand and the farmer made their way in the dark out to the oat field—neither one of them saying a word.

Finally the city slicker asked what kind of oats they were going to cut: wild oats or tamed oats. The farmer, a little surprised, asked what he meant. "Well," the young man said, "I was just wondering why we're sneaking up on 'em in the dark."

☆

There was a rural couple that on their day off went to the art exhibit in the city. It was an exhibit of modern, abstract art.

The husband walked up to the first picture, and he took a look at it. He looked from another angle, and then—well, he tried it from every angle and finally turned to his wife and said, "I want to buy it." She said, "You what? You want to buy it?"

He said, "Yes. It's the best darn picture of the farm situation I ever saw. No matter which way you look at it," he said, "it doesn't make sense."

☆

A good old boy had taken over some land down in a creek bottom. It was covered with rocks and brush and was pretty scraggly, and he went to work on it.

He worked and worked, and finally he had a garden that

was his pride and joy. So one Sunday morning after services he asked the minister if he wouldn't like to come out and see his garden.

Well, the minister arrived and he looked. He looked at the melons, and he said, "Oh, the Lord has certainly blessed this land." He looked at the corn, and he said, "My, my, the Lord sure has blessed this corn." He said, "My, what the Lord and you have managed to accomplish here." And he went on that way for about ten minutes.

The old boy finally said, "Reverend, I wish you could have seen this when the Lord was doing it by himself."

In one of Montana's early settlements there were two fellows who owned a general store.

One of them was a Spaniard, and the other one was a Frenchman, and neither of them could understand the language of the other. Now, I don't know how they made out, but it sort of reminds you of Congress and me, doesn't it?

☆

The actress Clara Bow once said of that famous Montana movie star Gary Cooper, "When he puts his arms around me, I feel like a horse."

Well, for a conservative president like me to have to put his arms around a multibillion-dollar deficit, it's like holding your nose and embracing a pig. And believe me that budget deficit is as slippery as a greased pig.

☆

There were three gentlemen who had departed this Earth and were standing at the great gates of heaven waiting for admittance.

One was a surgeon, one an engineer, the third an economist. They'd all been good, upright people, but it developed that there was only room inside for one.

So St. Peter said, "I'll tell you what, I'll pick the one who comes from the oldest profession."

The surgeon stepped right up and said, "Well, I'm your man. Right after God created Adam, he operated. He took a rib and created Eve, so surgery must be the oldest profession."

The engineer said, "No. You see, before God created Adam and Eve, he took the chaos that prevailed and built Earth in six days. So engineering had to precede surgery."

Then the economist spoke up. "Now hold on, who do you think created all that chaos?"

☆

There was a marine detachment that was sent to an army base for some airborne training. The young lieutenant who was explaining everything said that the plane would come over at about eight hundred feet. They would jump and would then assemble and rendezvous with other forces in the area.

When he finished, the marines there went into a kind of huddle. Pretty soon several of them as spokesmen went up to the lieutenant and said, "Lieutenant, could the plane maybe come over a little lower, say, at about five hundred feet?" Well, he explained, no, it couldn't because the parachutes wouldn't have time to open.

"Oh," they said, "we're wearing parachutes?"

☆

Some of my hardworking aides recommended against leaving the Capitol and coming all the way out here.

So to keep them happy I said, "Okay, let's flip a quarter to decide whether to visit your beautiful state or stay in Washington." And you know something? I had to flip fourteen times before it came out right . . .

Then I got them together and said, "Boys, we're going where the people think big and the sky's the limit." You know what I meant; they didn't. They all headed for Tip O'Neill's office.

☆

You know the story about the fellow who said to his friend, "I was sorry to hear that your wife ran off with the gardener." And his friend said, "Well, that's all right. I was going to fire him anyway."

When it comes to economy, that's about how scrambled the logic has been in recent years.

And scrambled thinking led us to a scrambled economic mess. Our critics are saying the economy is on its knees. Well, you know something? If the economy is on its knees, that's quite an improvement because two years ago it was flat on its back.

☆

A young Texan boy asked a stranger he'd just met if the man was from the great state of Texas. Seeing this, the kid's father took him aside and said, "Son, I want you always to remember one thing: If a man comes from Texas, he'll tell you without being asked, and if he doesn't come from Texas, there's no need to embarrass him."

☆

There was a Texan who was visiting a farmer up in Maine. The Texan asked this old boy about his farm and what might be the extent of his spread.

The old fellow said, "Well, it runs to that clump of trees and then over to that hill and then down to the creek and over to there. How big is your spread in Texas?"

The Texan looked at him and said, "Well, old-timer, sometimes I get in my car and drive for an hour and a half before I get to the boundary of my farm."

The old fellow from Maine looked at him for a minute and then said, "I know exactly what you mean. I had a car like that myself once."

☆

Mark Twain was on a steamer going across to Europe. In

the dining salon one night at dinner, someone at the table who wanted to impress him asked him to pass the sugar and then said, "Mr. Twain, don't you think it's unusual that sugar is the only word in our language in which *s-u* has the *shu* sound?"

And Twain said, "Are you sure?"

☆

I feel very much at home here in your lovely farm and dairy country. I'm a rancher myself. I take a little kidding now and then in Washington about our ranch.

But you know, even some midwesterners admit that cattle fit right into the California scene. They stand around all day in the sun, no clothes on, eating salad.

I just want to assure you that cows in California are the same as cows in Minnesota. Except, of course, in California they have their teeth capped.

☆

You know I've never been very good myself at fundraising. My friends tell me that's why I got in government, because we don't ask for it, we just take.

I remember the man who became the chairman of his small-town charity. Looking at the records, he went to a citizen of the town who had a six-figure income but who had never contributed to the town charity. He called his attention to this fact and said that the record showed that "you have this income and you've never contributed."

And he said, "Do your records also show that my brother was wounded in the war, permanently disabled and never able to work again? Do they show that my sister was widowed with several children, and there was no insurance, there was no means of subsistence?"

Kind of abashed, the chairman said, "Well, no, the records don't show that."

"Well," he said, "I don't give anything to them. Why should I give something to you?" ☆

Mr. Reagan was attending the annual dinner party of the White House News Photographers Association. It was a chance for the President and the photographers to poke fun, away from the demands of the job:

Now I've been told that this is all off the record and that the cameras are all off. Is that right? Because I've been waiting years to do this . . .

(At that point, the President jammed his thumbs in his ears and wiggled his fingers at the audience.)

I want to tell you, though, that Nancy and I had a bad moment when we came in here. You're all so beautifully dressed and dressed up that we thought we'd come to the wrong dinner. Usually you have a bag over your shoulder and you look a little rumpled, sort of like a fellow that's just checking out of a motel that he'd rather not be seen leaving.

But on the level, though, I like photographers. You don't ask questions. Can you imagine Sam Donaldson with a camera? As most of you would say, the thought makes me shutter . . .

I'm told that there's a feeling among photographers that journalists don't treat you well or as fairly as you'd like. Welcome to the club.

You know, I like your White House Photographers' motto: One picture is worth a thousand denials.

I know this isn't a partisan political affair. But I also know that you have wide-angle lenses that are wide enough to get all the Democratic presidential candidates in one shot. You just don't have a lens that's wide enough to get all their promises . . .

There are some things that you and I have in common in addition to being on the opposite ends of the camera. For you, the darkroom is a place to develop film. For me, it's a place Democrats use as a think tank.

But let's get serious for just a moment, and a moment is all I'm going to take.

On a newspaper or a magazine page, I always look at your work first, and so does everyone else. It's that still photo that captures the essence of the moment and sticks in our memory. If the written or broadcast media could capture the truth as consistently and accurately as you do, the American people might have a better perspective on the issues.

I do admire what you do. And I believe you do your job honestly and fairly. And that's the basis of our press freedoms.

And so I thank you for inviting us here this evening . . . and if you'll just remember, my best side is my right side—my far right side.

☆

I remember the first time I visited a nuclear power facility.

In one building they were showing me through, we put on felt boots and gowns and we went through.

Afterward, we had to peel all of it off. And there was a slot machine there in which you put your hands and your feet—and there were four dials that started ticking away measuring the amount of radioactivity that you might have picked up in your extremities.

The dials were all fine, except on my left hand. That dial kept on ticking, and it was getting up to where the numbers were red. So I was getting a little concerned. The manager of the plant looked over my shoulder and said, "Oh, your left hand. That always happens. That's the radium dial on your wristwatch."

I was very relieved. I was two hundred miles away from there when I realized—I don't have a radium dial.

Every once in a while I still put my head under the covers and look to see if my hand is lighting up.

☆

Mr. Reagan, still on the subject of nuclear power, joked about the two farmers talking:

One of them said to the other, "Where would you like to be in the the event of a nuclear explosion?" And the old boy said, "Some place where I could say, 'What was that?' "

☆

I heard of a fellow who had been unemployed for a long time and then finally found a job at a warehouse for fine china.

He'd only worked there a couple of days when he smashed a large oriental vase. The boss told him in no uncertain terms that the money would be deducted from his wages every week until the vase was paid for.

The fellow asked, "How much did it cost?" He was told $300, and the fellow cheered and said, "At last, I've found steady work."

☆

Mr. Reagan was on hand at the fortieth anniversary of the USO and Bob Hope's association with the USO. The two men traded one-liners all night. Here are a few of the President's:

I don't think any of us realize that there probably isn't anyone who loves his work as much as Bob Hope.

I discovered that once when he was up at our ranch and I took him over to show him our horses. Then I got a telephone call. When I came back he was doing a monologue to the horses. And they were laughing.

Of course his other love is golf. When we met tonight I said, "Hello, how are you?" And he said, "Hello, what's your handicap?" I said, "The Congress."

☆

I received a letter from an environmentalist the other day, and he was thanking me.

He said it's the first time he's ever been able to make his children behave. He now scares them into being good by telling 'em James Watt will get 'em.

Of course all the mail isn't that good. I've been getting some flack about ordering the production of the B-1. How did I

The President with Bob Hope, John Wayne, Dean Martin, Frank Sinatra

know it was an airplane? I thought it was a vitamin for the troops.

I never miss a chance to visit Philadelphia, America's historic treasure. For one thing, there aren't too many cities that have been around so much longer than I have.

And you know, your Ben Franklin once said, "Work as if you were to live a hundred years, pray as if you were to die tomorrow."

And ever since he told me that I've been doing just fine.

Mr. Reagan loves to keep up on Russian jokes. One of them is about an American and a Russian who were arguing about the differences between the two countries:

The American said, "Look, in my country I can walk into the Oval Office; I can hit the desk with my fist and say, 'President Reagan, I don't like the way you're governing the United States.'"

And the Russian said, "I can do that." The American said, "What?" He said, "I can walk into the Kremlin, into Brezhnev's office. I can pound Brezhnev's desk, and I can say, 'Mr. President, I don't like the way Ronald Reagan is governing the United States.'"

☆

Then there was the day Brezhnev first became president. He invited his elderly mother to come up and see his suite of offices in the Kremlin, and then put her in a limousine and drove her to his fabulous apartment there in Moscow.

And in both places not a word; she looked but said nothing. Then he put her in his helicopter and took her out to the country home in a forest outside Moscow. And again not a word.

Finally, he put her in his private jet and flew down to the shores of the Black Sea to see the marble palace which is known as his beach home.

At last she spoke. "Leonid, what if the Communists find out?"

☆

The Russian commissar went out to inspect a collective farm. He grabbed one of the workers there and asked him how things were and whether or not there were any complaints.

"Oh no, sir," he said. "I've never heard anyone around here complain about anything."

"Well," the commissar said, "what about the crops?"

"My comrade, the crops are better than ever."

"How about the potato harvest?" The farmer said, "If we piled all the potatoes harvested up in one pile, they'd reach the foot of God."

The commissar said, "This is the Soviet Union, there is no

God." The farmer said, "That's all right, there aren't any potatoes either."

☆

Mr. Reagan, at a GOP fundraiser, poked fun at the antics of politicians, quoting them at their finest:
One legislator began a speech with this statement, "Before I give you the benefit of my remarks, I'd like to know what we're talking about."

Then there was the one who announced, "Some of our friends wanted it in the bill; some of our friends wanted it out. And Jerry and I are going to stick with our friends."

Another warned, "From now on I'm watching everything you do with a fine-toothed comb."

And one gentleman said bluntly, "I don't think people appreciate how difficult it is to be a pawn of labor."

My own favorite is, "Mr. Speaker, what bill did we just pass?"

☆

Mr. Reagan, trying to make a point that you can have too much of a good thing:
There was a small town on a lake, and a young man there, named Elmer, went into business for himself selling fish to the local restaurant. But no one could figure out how Elmer managed to catch so many fish every day and deliver them on time to the restaurant.

And so the game warden asked his cousin, who happened to be the sheriff, to look into the matter. The sheriff asked Elmer to take him fishing, figuring he'd find out where this fabulous fishing hole was.

They rowed out to the middle of the lake. The sheriff cast his line. Elmer reached down in the tackle box and came up with a stick of dynamite, lit the fuse, and threw it in the water.

After the explosion, of course, the fish, by the hundreds, belly-up, came floating to the surface.

Well, the sheriff just looked at Elmer and said, "Do you realize you just committed a felony?"

Elmer reached into the tackle box, came up with another stick of dynamite, lit it, handed it to the sheriff, and said, "Did you come here to talk or fish?"

☆

Castro was making a speech to a large audience, and he said, "They accuse me of intervening in Angola." And a man going through the audience said, "Peanuts, popcorn." Castro said, "They say I'm intervening in Mozambique." And the same voice: "Peanuts, popcorn." And he said, "They say I'm intervening in Nicaragua." "Peanuts, popcorn."

By this time Castro was boiling mad, and he said, "Bring me that man who is shouting peanuts and popcorn, and I'll kick him all the way to Miami."

And everybody in the crowd started shouting, "Peanuts, popcorn."

☆

A few years back, at a military base out west, some of the men had gotten together a poker game, which was strictly against the rules.

Well, the MPs were tipped off and raided the barracks. The four poker players just managed to hide the cards and chips in time. When the police got there, they were sitting at an empty table staring innocently at each other. The MP sergeant asked each in turn if he'd been gambling.

The soldier bit his lip and replied, "No, Sarge, I haven't been gambling."

The sailor paused, silently asked the Lord's forgiveness, and also said he wasn't gambling. And the airman answered the same way.

That brought them to the marine, and they asked if he'd been gambling. The marine looked the cop right dead in the eye and asked, "Who with?"

☆

Mr. Reagan, speaking to entrepreneurs about risk-taking and optimism:

50

There was the fellow whose friend was so successful in business that he was opening up a new branch office. He decided to send a floral arrangement for the grand opening. When he got there, he was shocked to find that the wreath that was delivered bore the inscription: Rest in peace.

He was angry, and on the way home he stopped at the flower shop to complain. He was going at it, and the florist said, "Wait a minute. Just look at it this way: Somewhere in the land today a man was buried under a wreath that said, 'Good luck in your new location.'"

☆

There was a secret agent overseas in Ireland. There was an emergency, and it was necessary to contact him right away. So they called in another agent and said, "Now, you go there to find him. His name is Murphy, and your recognition will be to say, ' 'Tis a fair day, but it'll be lovelier this evening.'"

So he went to this little town in Ireland, into the pub, elbowed himself up to the bar, ordered a drink, and then said to the bartender, "How would I get in touch with Murphy?"

The bartender says, "Well, if it's Murphy the farmer you want, it's two miles down the road, and it's the farm on the left. If it's Murphy the bootmaker, he's on the second floor of the building across the street. And," he says, "my name is Murphy."

So the agent picked up the drink and he said, "Well, 'tis a fair day, but it'll be lovelier this evening."

"Oh," he said, "it's Murphy the spy you want. Well, he's . . ."

☆

It's great to get out of the White House and have some fun once in a while. You know, I once attended an Italian-American festival where everyone was having a joyous time.

There was such life and vitality and all kinds of delicious foods, and I said to the man next to me, "If anyone felt lonely, this is the place to be." "That's true," he said. "No one can be lonely while eating spaghetti. It takes so much attention."

51

So, when I think of Italian families, I never think of loneliness but of warm kitchens and even warmer love.

One family was living in a little apartment but decided to move to a big house in the country. A friend said to the twelve-year-old son, Tony, "How do you like your new house?" And he said, "We love it. I have my own room. My brother has his own room. My sisters have their own rooms. But poor Mom, she's still in with Dad."

Too often federal intrusiveness has become a part of the problem, not the solution.

I'm reminded of the story about a young student who handed in a test paper riddled with errors, and his teacher asked him how one person could make so many mistakes. And he said, "One person didn't. My father helped me."

Well, maybe the federal government has helped local governments make some mistakes.

I've often wondered about the shyness of some of us in the West about standing for those ideals that have done so much for the plight of man and the hardships of our imperfect world.

This reluctance to use the vast resources at our command reminds me of the elderly lady whose home was bombed in the Blitz.

As the rescuers moved about, they found a bottle of brandy she'd stored behind the staircase, which was all that was left standing.

Since she was barely conscious, one of the workers pulled the cork to give her a taste of it.

She came around immediately and said, "Here now, put it back. That's for emergencies."

For too many years we've been told that the only logical place to turn for help of any kind is Washington.

I know that many of the programs that have been proposed over the past had the best of intentions—to help people. But when you set out to help people, you'd better be sure of what you're doing. And they weren't all that sure.

They make me think of the fellow riding a motorcycle on a cold, winter day, and the wind was coming through the buttonholes on his leather jacket and chilling him.

So he stopped, got off, turned the jacket around, and put it on backward. Well, now he was all right from the cold, but his arm movements were kind of restricted. A little while later he hit a patch of ice and skidded into a tree.

The police got there, elbowed their way through the crowd that had gathered, and asked, "What happened?" They said, "We don't know. When we got here he seemed to be all right, but by the time we had his head turned around straight, he was dead."

☆

The strength of the Solidarity movement in Poland demonstrates the truth told in an underground joke in the Soviet Union. It is that the Soviet Union would remain a one-party nation even if an opposition party were permitted because everyone would join the opposition party.

☆

You know, I'm beginning to believe some of those stories about Texas, especially that one about the good old boy from Kentucky.

He was bragging that they had enough gold in Fort Knox to build a six-foot-tall solid gold fence all the way around Texas.

And the Texan he was talking to said, "Yeah, well, you build it, and we'll buy it."

☆

Madison Avenue and those advertising agencies found out what we westerners have always known and loved about western sports, western men, and cowgirls.

Of course, there is one advertisement that I've never quite

understood. That's the TV ad about the cowboy out there in the middle of a herd of cattle, and the caption on the picture is: Come to where the flavor is.

☆

A fellow fell off a cliff. As he was falling he grabbed a limb sticking out the side of the cliff and looked down three hundred feet to the canyon floor below. Then he looked up and said, "Lord, if there's anyone up there, give me faith. Tell me what to do."

And a voice from the heavens said, "If you have faith, let go."

He looked down at the canyon floor and then took another look up and said, "Is there anyone else up there?"

☆

A newspaper photographer was called in by his editor and told of a raging fire. The photographer's assignment was to rush down to the local airport, board a waiting plane, go out and get some pictures of the fire, and be back in time for the afternoon edition.

Well, he raced down the freeway, broke all the traffic laws, got to the airport, drove his car to the end of the runway, and sure enough, there was a plane revving up its engines, ready to go.

He jumped in the plane shouting, "Let's go!" and they were off. At about five thousand feet he began getting his camera out of the bag and told the fellow flying the plane to get him over the fire so he could get his pictures and get back to the paper.

From the other side of the cockpit there was a deafening silence, and then he heard the words he will always remember: "Aren't you the instructor?"

☆

Some politicians are kind of like the two campers who were hiking and spotted a grizzly bear coming over the hill, headed right for them.

One of them reached into his pack as quick as he could, pulled out a pair of tennis shoes, sat down, and started putting on the tennis shoes.

The other looked at him and said, "You don't mean you think you can outrun a grizzly?"

The fellow with the tennis shoes stood up and said, "I don't have to outrun the grizzly; I just have to outrun you."

☆

Sometimes government programs remind me of the country preacher who called on a town one hundred miles from his own. He went there for a revival meeting.

Going to church, he noticed a man seated on the porch of a little country store who was from his own hometown, a fellow who was known for his drinking.

The minister went up to him and asked him what he was doing so far from home. "Preacher," he said, "beer is five cents a bottle cheaper here."

The minister told him that it didn't make much sense, what with the expense of traveling all that way and back, and the price of lodging and whatnot.

The drinker thought for a moment and then replied, "Preacher, I'm not stupid. I just sit here until I show a profit."

☆

I once addressed a farm group in Las Vegas, Nevada. One of those fellows who was in Vegas for the action saw me, recognized me, and said, "What are you doing here?" So I told him. "Well," he says, "what's a bunch of farmers doing in Las Vegas?"

That was a straight line I couldn't ignore. I said, "Buster, they're in an occupation that makes a Las Vegas crap table look like a guaranteed annual income."

☆

An evangelical minister and a politician arrived at heaven's gate one day together. St. Peter, after handling all the formalities, took them in hand to show them where their new quarters would be. He took them to a small, single room with a bed, a chair, and a table, and said this was for the clergyman.

Well, the politician was a little worried about what might be in store for him. He couldn't believe it when St. Peter stopped in front of a beautiful mansion with lovely grounds and many servants, and told him that these would be his quarters.

The politician couldn't help but ask, "But wait—there's something wrong. How do I get a mansion while that good and holy man only gets a single room?"

And St. Peter said, "You have to understand how things are up here. We've got thousands and thousands of clergy. You're the first politician who ever made it."

☆

A preacher-friend of mine from Oklahoma taught me the lesson of brevity in a speech. He recalled his first appearance in the pulpit. He had worked for weeks on this first sermon, which he was to give at an evening service in a little country church.

Well, he stood up in the pulpit that night and looked out at an empty church, except for one lone little fellow sitting down there in all the empty pews.

So after the music, he went down and said, "Look, my friend, I'm just a young preacher getting started. You seem to be the only member of the congregation who showed up. What about it, should I go through with it?"

The fellow said, "Well, I'm a little old cowpoke out here in Oklahoma. I don't know much about that sort of thing, but I do know this: If I loaded up a truckload of hay, took it out to the prairie, and only one cow showed up, I'd feed her."

The preacher took that as a cue, got back up in the pulpit, and an hour and a half later said, "Amen." He then went back down and said, "My friend, you seem to have stuck with me. And like I told you, I'm a young preacher getting started. Tell me what you thought."

"Well," he says, "like I told you, I don't know about that sort of thing, but I do know this: If I loaded up a truckload of hay, took it out on the prairie, and only one cow showed up, I sure wouldn't give her the whole load."

☆

We conservatives, if we mean to continue governing, must realize that it will not always be so easy to put the blame on the past for our national difficulties.

You know, one day the great baseball manager Frankie Frisch sent a rookie out to play center field. The rookie promptly dropped the first fly ball that was hit to him. On the next play he let a grounder go between his feet and then threw the ball to the wrong base.

Frankie stormed out of the dugout, took the glove away from him, and said, "I'll show you how to play this position." Well, the next batter slammed a line drive right over second base. Frankie came in on it, missed it completely, fell down when he tried to chase it, threw down the glove, and yelled at the rookie, "You've got center field so screwed up, nobody can play it."

☆

Mr. Reagan had just been introduced by Interior Secretary James Watt. Mr. Watt's speech was one of his finest ever, and his line, "Let Reagan be Reagan," had the partisan crowd of Reagan true-believers on their feet and cheering:

I thank you very much, except I feel a little bit like the last living survivor of the Johnstown flood who finally came to the end of his days. St. Peter greeted him as a newcomer and told him that there were some old-timers there who would like to gather and hear the latest word from Earth, and did he have anything interesting to contribute?

He thought for a minute, then explained how he'd been quite a feature on the mashed-potato circuit with his tales of the Johnstown flood. "Oh," St. Peter said, "I know they'll like that." He brought the newcomer in, introduced him, and said he had something very interesting to say. And then, just as he turned to leave, he whispered in the fellow's ear, "That man second from the left in the first row—his name is Noah."

☆

Mr. Reagan, later in the same speech to his supporters, talked about optimism:

A man had two sons, and he was very disturbed about them. One was a pessimist beyond recall, and the other was an optimist beyond reason. He talked to a child psychiatrist who made a suggestion. He said, "I think we can fix that. We'll get a room, and we'll fill it with the most wonderful toys any boy ever had. And we'll put the pessimist in, and when he finds out the toys are for him, he'll get over being a pessimist."

The father said, "What will you do about the optimist?"

"Well," he said, "I have a friend who has a racing stable, and they clean out the stalls every morning. And," he said, "I can get quite an amount of that substance. We'll put that in another room, and when the optimist who's seen his brother get all the toys is then shown his own room, he'll get over it."

Well, they showed each boy his room and waited five minutes. When they opened the door, the pessimist was crying as if his heart would break. He said, "I know somebody's going to come in and take these away from me."

Then they went down to the other room and opened the door, and there was the kid happy as a clam, throwing that stuff over his shoulder as fast as he could. They said, "What are you doing?" And he said, "There's got to be a pony in here somewhere."   ☆

Mr. Reagan, talking about New Mexico and her independent folk:

A prospector once came down out of those mountains, and when he arrived in civilization, he announced that he'd been up there for forty years.

The fellow he was saying this to said, "You mean you've been up in the mountains for forty years looking for gold?" And he says, "Nope, I was only looking for gold for one year. The other thirty-nine I was looking for my burro."

☆

Mr. Reagan, speaking to a group of crusty old newspaper reporters, tried to illustrate how hard they are to impress:

You know, in the old days of vaudeville, it used to be that ambitious young vaudevillians would go into an empty theater and try out in front of a blasé booking agent who'd be sitting there in one of the front seats with a cigar, all alone in the theater, watching them do their act—and he was very hard to please.

One young fellow walked out to center stage. The agent asked him what he did, and the kid just took off and flew around the whole theater—made a couple of circles clear up to the ceiling, came back down, and landed back at center stage.

The agent says, "What else do you do besides bird imitations?"

☆

In spite of all the stories you hear on television, the truth is that this administration will devote more money to health care than any administration in history. It may come as a surprise, but 49 million elderly, poor, and disabled Americans will be served through Medicare and Medicaid in 1984. That's 3 million more than in 1980.

With this kind of solid record, you can see why I get a little irritated with our critics. They remind me of the hypochondriac who was complaining to the doctor. He said, "My left

59

arm hurts me, also my left foot, and my back. Oh, and there's my hip and, oh, yes, my neck."

Well, the doctor muttered something to himself and then sat him down, crossed his legs, and tapped him with the little rubber hammer. Doc says, "How are you now?" And he says, "Now my knee hurts too."

☆

What the Democrats had done to this country reminds me of the little girl who said to her mother, "You know that beautiful jug you told me had been handed down in our family from generation to generation?" And her mother said, "Yes, what about it?" She said, "Well, this generation just dropped it."

☆

An old preacher was giving some advice to a young preacher. He said, "You know, sometimes on Sunday morning they'll begin to nod off." And he says, "I've found a way to wake them up. Right in my sermon when I see them beginning to doze, I say, 'Last night I held in my arms a woman who is the wife of another man.' Then, when they look at me startled, I say, 'It was my dear mother.'"

Well, the young preacher took that to heart, and a few weeks later, sure enough, some in the congregation were dozing off. He remembered the advice, and he said, "Last night I held in my arms a woman who is the wife of another man." They all looked at him, and everyone was awake. And he says, "I can't remember who it was."

4 ☆ "It Takes All Kinds of Jelly Beans"

General Sherman once said that "if forced to choose between the penitentiary and the White House for four years, I would say the penitentiary, thank you."

Now, I wouldn't go that far, but I will admit there have been days that fit his description of war when he said, "War is . . ."

☆

Mr. Reagan was asked by friends what surprised him most about the White House:

The biggest surprises are the leaks. I'll tell you, I've gotten so that I address some things in cabinet meetings to the chandelier. I'm sure it must have a microphone.

☆

The cynics may call it corny, but this way of life we all cherish is best summed up in three simple words: The American Dream.

☆

Just the other day I read where some astronomers predict that one of the largest stars in the Milky Way is going to explode sometime in the next ten thousand years. And the fellow who was writing the story said they weren't quite sure when in these ten thousand years the blow-up would take place, but it would be the result of our economic recovery program.

☆

Jesse Helms wants me to move to the right; Lowell Weicker wants me to move to the left: Teddy Kennedy wants me to move back to California.

☆

It's not true that the Moral Majority has been trying to exert undo influence on me. That rumor started recently when Jerry Falwell called me with a suggestion for ambassador to Iran: the publisher of *Penthouse*.

☆

Lately I've been eyeing a tradition from ancient Greece. History has it that there was a city-stage there with a custom that if anyone wanted to suggest a government program, he did so standing on a chair with a noose around his neck.

If the people liked the idea, they took the noose off. And if they didn't, they took the chair away.

☆

Mr. Reagan was meeting with the Washington Redskins after their 1983 Super Bowl championship:
Last week I was thinking of asking Riggins if he might change the spelling of his name a little bit so that it had an *ea* in it.

But now, would he mind if I changed my spelling so that it has an *i* and a couple of *g*'s in it?

☆

There's an old economic axiom, still true today, that says, "If people are not allowed to earn more by producing more, then more will not be produced."

That's why our tax incentives are critical to sustaining economic recovery.

☆

I realize there's a theory that good news isn't good for the ratings, but I would like to suggest to the media that during National Volunteer Week they give attention to America's heroic private sector initiatives. Then, if the ratings go down, they can go back to the bad news.

☆

For many years, rather than bringing spending down closer to revenues, government simply raised revenues the sneaky way. It used inflation to push every working family in America toward higher and higher tax brackets. Ironically, they call this progressive, compassionate, and fair.

It reminds me of Samuel Johnson's comment about a fellow who couldn't see the difference between virtue and vice: "When he leaves, count the spoons."

Back in the days before we had satellites and electronic hookups, Thomas Jefferson said, "Were it left to me to decide whether we should have a government without newspapers or newspapers without a government, I should not hesitate a moment to prefer the latter."

Well now, I couldn't help noticing something about that kind remark Jefferson made about the press. He made it before he was president.

☆

Once during the campaign some fellow said to me that he didn't think I was working very hard. He said, "You've got too good a tan." And I said, "Well, I've been doing a lot of outdoor rallies." And then he said, "Well, you talk too long then."

☆

We will not let the doom criers and the scaremongers frighten our citizens and subvert recovery.

All they offer is a return to their failed policies of the past: more big spending, more big taxing, more regulations, more meddling, and more make-work—more big government coming through the windows, underneath the door, and down the chimney.

☆

You know, when we got to Washington, this country was in the fast lane headed toward economic oblivion.

The folks who'd been at the wheel were more reckless than the Dukes of Hazzard—they'd been spending, taxing, inflating, and borrowing as if there were no tomorrow.

☆

Mr. Reagan was paying tribute to National Amateur Baseball Month, hitting the ball around the Rose Garden:

Well, this is more fun than being president. I really do love baseball, and I wish we could do this out on the lawn every day.

I wouldn't even complain if a stray ball came through the Oval Office window now and then. . . .

Baseball, of course, is our national pastime, that is if you discount political campaigning. That sign of spring is nine guys galloping out on the field—the Democratic presidential candidates. No runs, no hits, just errors.

Our party is going to be in good shape by 1984. We'll do well because of what you might call the "Republican Strategic Triad." That's fundraising ability, nuts and bolts organization, and talented candidates.

Several years ago, while I was still governor of California, after a tragic assassination in this country, Secret Service agents were assigned to several of us in public office.

On weekends, when I could, I liked to get out to the ranch and do a little target shooting and plinking at tin cans. They liked to keep their hand in too. So together we would go down to the woods and do some target shooting.

One day I mentioned that I had read an article on shooting from the hip. And they said, "Oh, yes, we have to do that."

One of them set a tin can up, and I went into a crouch and blazed away, but the can was unhit. Then one of them stepped up and, standing erect, took his turn. I said, "Well, wait a minute. You didn't crouch."

And he sort of pebble-pushed there for a minute. He didn't know quite how to answer me, and he said, "Well . . ." Finally he mumbled, "We lose our rating if we crouch." And I said, "Well, I don't understand. The article said . . ."

The unit chief took me aside and said, "Governor, if we're ever shooting at anyone, we're between him and his target."

It was quite an awakening.

☆

Ronald Reagan, speaking to champions of American sport:
If it had not been for football, track, and swimming, I might not have been able to go to college.

We didn't have athletic scholarships in those days; we had to do things like wind the clock in the gym. But I loved it when it was plain and simple and honorable. . . .

Actually, there was a rule—you could employ someone as an athletic instructor and still leave him eligible to play.

In my senior year, on the starting eleven, there were seven P.E. instructors, and I was the swimming coach . . . for eight years.

I didn't know much about As and Bs scholastically; the eligibility requirement was a C average, and that became my top goal.

I couldn't play baseball because I couldn't see well enough. That's why I turned to football; the ball was bigger, and so were the fellows.

☆

Mr. Reagan, following a meeting with the Queen of England in California:
I pointed out to her that if those first settlers to this country had only come across the Pacific instead of the Atlantic, the Capitol would today be in California. . . .

It's just as well because the rest of the country would never have been developed.

☆

Mr. Reagan, still in California:
I wish one thing about George Washington. He set so many precedents, why didn't he set one that the Capitol would henceforth be where the president lived?

☆

We've been proposing lower spending and taxes; doing that in Washington is a little like getting between the pig and the bucket—you get buffeted about a bit.

When we came into office, we rooted out waste and fraud that was running rampant—the federal government was still sending Social Security checks to thousands of people who had been dead for as much as seven years.

Now, I've heard of cradle to grave security, but cradle to Pearly Gates is something else.

Who said you can't take it with you?

Mr. Reagan, returning to his alma mater, Eureka College, to deliver the commencement address:

I only came back here to clean out my gym locker.

But I am excited to receive this honorary degree, since I had always figured that the first one was honorary.

Mr. Reagan's economic recovery program had been in place only a few weeks when the critics pronounced it a failure. The President found a newspaper cartoon that summed up his sentiments and passed it around the dinner table. It showed a TV reporter saying:

"And so it seems clear to this reporter that Reaganomics has failed, failed to thrive in a climate of optimism, failed to blossom into a viable economic alternative, failed to bear the fruit of prosperity—at least in these first five disappointing minutes."

When we took office, federal spending was growing at a rate that was steep enough to make a mountain goat dizzy. And the problem was that the Democrats genuinely believed—the poor misguided things, they still believe—that money can buy happiness.

Our international trading partners and we are in the same trading boat. If one partner shoots a hole in the bottom of the boat, does it make sense for the other partner to shoot another hole in the boat?

Some people say yes and call it getting tough. I call it getting wet.

☆

Mr. Reagan was the guest speaker at the tenth anniversary of the Heritage Foundation, the respected conservative think-tank. After being introduced by Joseph Coors, the President said:

Actually, I was a little surprised by the warmth of Joe's introduction. There is a certain coolness between Joe and me tonight. When I arrived here, I said, "Joe, it's been a long, hard day in the Oval Office, but now it's Miller time."

That's when he showed me his Mondale button.

But seriously, I'm delighted to be here at Heritage. I remember back in the days when a conservative intellectual was considered a contradiction in terms—you know, like a thrifty liberal, modest government, penny-pinching congressman.

☆

Mr. Reagan was asked what surprised him most about living in the White House:

It's going to work and home again in an elevator, and sometimes you get a little claustrophobia.

The quarters are beautiful, and it's very fine living. But every once in a while you do look out the window and see people walking by, and you say, "You know something that they can do and I can't? I can't just walk down to the corner drugstore and pick out a birthday card or magazine or something."

And so you go out to Camp David and get it out of your system.

☆

Mr. Reagan was next asked about his hair and whether he has changed his style:

I saw an article that said I had changed. They showed two different pictures of me. Well, the one was taken on a windy day outdoors, and the other one was taken with my hair combed.

Incidentally, I just washed my hair the night before last, so it's a little fluffy right now. The only thing that happened to me was, last winter, without my realizing it, my barber was letting it get a little longer than I like. And I took him to task and said, "Crop it the way it was."

It's the same haircut. I'm too hold to change my haircut now.

☆

Our view of government is essentially that of our Founding Fathers—that government is the servant, not the master; that it was meant to maintain order, to protect our nation's safety. But otherwise, in the words of that noted political philosopher, schnozzle Jimmy Durante, "Don't put no constrictions on da people; leave 'em da heck alone."

A word or two about *National Review*'s editor, Bill Buckley. And unlike Bill, I'll try to keep my words to single syllables, or at the worst only two.

I've often thought when I've been faced with memorandums from deep within the bowels of the bureaucracy what I wouldn't give to have Bill as an interpreter.

You know, a fellow comes in, stands in front of your desk, hands you a memorandum, and he stays there and waits while you read it. And so you read: "Action-oriented orchestration, innovation, inputs generated by escalation of meaningful, indigenous decision-making dialog, focusing on multilinked problem complexes, can maximize the vital thrust toward nonalienated and viable urban infrastructure."

I take a chance and say, "Let's try busing."

If he walks away, I know I guessed right.

☆

There are some things currently sweeping the country that I haven't had time to get familiar with—Pac Man, for example.

I asked about him, though, and somebody told me it was a round thing that gobbled up money.

I thought that was Tip O'Neill.

☆

I often get weary of the great seers and prophets in the financial and political worlds, some optimistic, some pessimistic, who, even if they don't know how to predict accurately, at least know how to predict often.

It reminds me of the sweet revenge that one businessman had recently when he told a company economist who was jumping out of the upper-story window, "Don't worry, Herb, you'll be bottoming out soon."

☆

Mr. Reagan was asked by a People *magazine reporter if his bullet-proof shirt or jacket hangs in the family quarters or whether the Secret Service keeps it some place else.*

MR. REAGAN: No, no. They keep it. And they come with it in hand, and they kind of come in flinching because they know I don't accept it with good grace.

REPORTER: What do you say when they put it on you?

MR. REAGAN: Oh, even an occasional unprintable word.

REPORTER: Is it bulky or heavy?

MR. REAGAN: Well, it's bulky. And I work so hard in the gym. Everybody will think I'm getting fat.

Mr. Reagan was later joking around with his political adviser who keeps his athlete's body in top shape. The aide asked Mr. Reagan what was his proudest accomplishment in office:

Well, working out every day, I've added an inch to my chest and a half-inch to my arms.

Mr. Reagan was swearing in the Chairman of the Commodity Futures Trading Commission when he felt a story coming on:
You know, that brings me to a story—almost everything does. Maybe I've told this story before, but then you'll just have to hear it again because life not only begins at age forty, but so does lumbago and the tendency to tell the same story over and over again.

Once upon a time you put money in your purse and went to the market to buy a bagful of groceries. Now you take a bag of money, go to the market, and bring the groceries home in your purse.

These are exciting times, the shuttle Columbia has been orbiting the Earth, Senator Glenn is in orbit around New Hampshire, and the federal budget is off somewhere in the wild blue yonder.

Mr. Reagan, speaking to a gathering of his federal appointees:
As the old saying goes, "When you're up to your armpits in alligators, it's sometimes hard to remember that your original intention was to drain the swamp."

I'm an optimist. If I wasn't, I never would have left the ranch to come here in the first place.
There is a simple definition for an optimist and a pessimist. An optimist asks, "Will you please pass the cream?" A pessimist says, "Is there any milk in that pitcher?"

My age doesn't bother me at all; Moses was 80 when God commissioned him for public service, and he lived to be 120.

Abraham was 100 and his wife Sarah 90 when they did something truly amazing—and he lived to be 175.

Just imagine if he had put $2,000 a year in his IRA account.

I recall earlier in the year we were in the middle of an intense partisan debate, and I invited one of the opposing senators to my office for a chat.

We both deeply believed what we were espousing, but we were on opposite sides. When we finished talking, as he rose, he said, "I'm going out of here, and I'm doing some praying." And I said, "Well, if you get a busy signal, it's me there ahead of you."

We've put in place an economic program that is based on sound economic theory, not political expediency. We will not play hopscotch economics, jumping here and there as the daily situation changes.

To the paid political complainers, let me say as politely as I can, "Put up or shut up."

Two partners decided to take the day off and go fishing. They'd rowed out into the middle of the lake, baited the hooks, and were waiting for the first bite when all of a sudden one of them said, "Sam, oh my gosh! We forgot to close the safe."

"So what," said Sam, "we're both here, aren't we?"

For too long that's the kind of partnership the federal government and the states have had. Neither really trusted the other, but Washington has been dipping into the cash drawer when the states weren't looking.

Official Washington's fascination with passing trends and one-day headlines can sometimes cause serious problems—like leaks. Before we even announced the giveaway of surplus cheese, the warehouse mice had hired a lobbyist.

Not too long ago Senator Kennedy paid a tribute to former Governor and Ambassador Averell Harriman, who was celebrating a birthday in his nineties. Kennedy said that Ambassador Harriman's age was only one-half as old as Ronald Reagan's ideas.

Well, you know, he's absolutely right! The United States Constitution is almost two hundred years old, and that's where I'm proud to get my ideas.

We've cut the number of new pages in the *Federal Register*, where the regulations are published, by twenty-three thousand pages. As George Bush likes to say, we're trying to get it down from the size of a copy of *War and Peace* to that of an issue of *Atlantic Monthly*.

I've been trying to get him to say *National Review*.

Just as Americans have spotted the dawn of a new age—strong growth without a return to runaway inflation and interest rates—the guardians of a graveyard philosophy want to resurrect ideas which should remain dead and buried for all time.

They have a kind of layaway plan for our lives that never changes. It's called: Americans make, government takes.

Thirty years ago, Speaker O'Neill, already a political veteran, was elected to Congress. Now, I was still in the movies in those days—but believe me, *Bedtime for Bonzo* made more sense than what they were doing in Washington.

I feel sorry for some Democratic congressmen. I hear they've been going home after a long day at the office, try to go to sleep, and the first thing you know, they're having nightmares that the money they're spending is their own.

Mr. Reagan, meeting with the Los Angeles Raiders following their 1984 Super Bowl Championship:
Congratulations, Coach Flores, but you've caused me some problems. I've already received a call from Moscow. They think that Marcus Allen is a new secret weapon, and they insist that we dismantle it.

But seriously, you've given me an idea. If you'd turn your team over to us, we'd put them in silos and we wouldn't have to build the MX missile.

Democratic candidates used to encourage people to work for their country—you know, "Ask not what your country can do for you, ask what you can do for your country."

Well, a few weeks after that inspirational message they introduced twenty-nine new spending programs of what the country could do for the people.

5 ★ "Well, Thank You, Thank You Very Much"

Thank you for that warm greeting and applause, but since that applause is coming from veterans, I have to ask, Is it for how I'm doing my job or how I'm doing on the late show in *Hellcats in the Navy?*

☆

Mrs. Reagan:
I've been asked to introduce my husband. I don't think I've

ever been asked to do that before. He looks pretty confident that I'm going to give him a good introduction, doesn't he?

I'll tell you a little secret. He didn't look so confident when I was going to introduce him to my father.

But instead of introducing the dynamic leader that we all admire, I'd like to present a kind, loving husband, a pushover of a father, and the President of the United States.

Mr. Reagan:

I want you all to know that she isn't really that much taller than me. It's just that they've taken away the box she was standing on.

☆

Mr. Reagan had been briefing reporters on defense matters and was looking for a way to change the subject to his economic recovery program:

You know, this is a little like the fellow at the wedding when the minister got to the portion of the ceremony where he said, "If anyone can show just cause why these two should not be wed, let him speak now or forever hold his peace."

And in the moment of silence that followed, a voice in the back said, "Well, if no one wants to say nothing about the bride and groom, I'd like to say a few words about my home state of Texas."

So I'm going to say it: After nineteen deficits in the last twenty years, with a national debt of nearly a trillion dollars, we face a choice of drastic action or inviting economic calamity.

☆

Mr. Reagan had learned that a group of businesswomen had mistakenly been turned away from a scheduled tour of the White House. Red-faced, the President went out of his way to speak to the ladies at their afternoon meeting:

When I found out what happened, I called and said I was standing on the third-floor ledge of the White House, prepared to jump.

Of course, I didn't. . . .

But I am going back to the White House, find out who was responsible, put them on the window ledge, and shove.

☆

Ladies and gentlemen, if suddenly in the midst of my remarks you see some individuals getting up and leaving, don't think them rude. They are congressmen going to the House because there is a vote coming up shortly. . . .

All those who are against my side in the vote stay here.

☆

I have to apologize for keeping you waiting. It happens a lot, you know, and sometimes I wonder if there isn't some other way, without making it sound that way, if in the announcement they couldn't say, "The late President of the United States."

☆

It's a pleasure to help open this American Cowboy Exhibit at the Library of Congress. This may mark the beginning of a new era in Washington—some sorely needed horse sense has finally come to Capitol Hill.

☆

Welcome to the White House. Nancy and I manage to be very happy here, in spite of having a hundred MXs in the basement.

☆

I want to let you in on a little secret. I have a horror of people that interrupt dessert, having been on the mashed-potato circuit for so many years. And I'm a dessert man.

Usually, the fellow stands up and starts introducing you just about the time they put the dessert down.

And you stand there talking, looking down at it as it melts. So, eat.

☆

Mr. Reagan, speaking to the shuttle astronauts just before their space walk:
Well now, wait till I get my hat, and I'll go with you.

☆

Mr. Reagan, upon hearing a newsman slip up and say, "Mr. Secretary, uh, Mr. President, uh, excuse me . . ."
Gee, I thought for a minute I'd lost my job.

☆

Mr. Reagan, speaking to the leaders of charitable groups:
I hear the cynics who have given up on our country. They're so quick to run down America, to find fault with everyone but themselves. To hear them talk, no one feels concern for a fellow citizen or cares about our future.

Sometimes they give the impression the United States is dying from cirrhosis of the giver.

☆

Mr. Reagan was reviewing a presentation of the famed Austrian Lippizäners:
They are touring the United States with these magnificent Lippizäner horses. We have only seen just a tiny bit of what they actually do in their exhibitions.

It is particularly fitting that this is the first time this has ever happened on the White House lawn—

(At this point Mr. Reagan was interrupted when the horses whinnied.)

Just a minute! I know I'm talking too long, I'll make it short. . . .

☆

I am happy to be here on behalf of New Mexico's Republican party.

It feels good to be here in the land of enchantment and out of the land of disenchantment there on the banks of the Potomac.

Mr. Reagan, speaking before the Oklahoma state legislature:
The people who settled here not only endured, they triumphed. Some who've never lived in this state often wonder why, with a population of only three million, you can produce such great football teams.

Well, after overcoming tornadoes, floods, drought, and Oklahoma winters, totin' a ball down a field a hundred yards just isn't such a hard job, even if there are eleven guys trying to stop you.

Delighted to have you all here this morning. Maybe some of you noticed the helicopter was on the lawn in case my reception was somewhat different—we're departing soon to make sure the West Coast is still attached.

Mr. Reagan, at a luncheon hosted by the Irish ambassador:
Well, I came not bearing gifts of such value, but I did bring a Waterford glass filled completely with green jelly beans.

☆

Mr. Reagan, making the point to conservatives that they should keep after him to keep his promises:
I hope you'll be like the mother of the young lad in camp when the camp director told her that he was going to have to discipline her son. And she said, "Well, don't be too hard on him. He's very sensitive. Slap the boy next to him, and that will scare Irving."

☆

Mr. Reagan was recovering from the attempt on his life, so George Bush delivered a scheduled speech to a group of congressional leaders:
You know, being asked to substitute for President Reagan

Vice President George Bush

as a guest speaker at a gathering of Republicans is like pinch-hitting for George Brett out there in Kansas City.

I'm the fifth president of the United States to address a Notre Dame commencement.

I'll try not to belabor you with some of the standard rhetoric that is beloved of graduation speakers. For example, I'm not going to tell you that "you know more today than you've ever known or that you will ever know again."

The other standby is, "When I was fourteen, I didn't think my father knew anything. By the time I was twenty-one, I was amazed at how much the old gentleman had learned in seven years."

And then, of course, the traditional one is that "a university like this is a storehouse of knowledge because the freshmen bring so much in and the seniors take so little away."

☆

Let me say on behalf of Nancy, who couldn't be here but wanted to be—she has a schedule too. I used to just come home, open the front door, and say, "I'm home." Now I come home, look through 132 rooms, and then look at her schedule—to know where she is.

☆

Mr. Reagan, toasting German Chancellor Schmidt:
We've discussed significant issues that affect us—our NATO and security commitments, our economic and foreign policies . . . I must admit, though, that one important matter was left off our agenda. I had hoped that we could resolve once and for all the relative advantages of Rhine wines versus California wines.

☆

Mr. Reagan, before the Indiana state legislature:
If the federal Government had been around when the Creator was putting His hand to this state, Indiana wouldn't be here. It'd still be waiting for an environmental impact statement.

☆

In the business that I used to be in, if you didn't sing or dance, you wound up as an after-dinner speaker—so here I am.

☆

The thing I like about speaking before doctors is that you generate as many anecdotes as do politicians. . . .

Like the one about the fellow who went to the hospital for a complete checkup, very depressed, and said to the doctor, "I look in the mirror, I'm a mess. My jowls are sagging. I have blotches all over my face. My hair has fallen out. I feel ugly. What is it?" And the doctor said, "I don't know what it is, but your eyesight is perfect."

I really have to apologize for being late today—I don't even know how to explain. What scares me is that one of the butlers who has been here for many, many years told me that this has never, ever happened.

We've been between here and the floor below—stuck in the elevator.

☆

Mr. Reagan was speaking before the Building and Construction Trades Department of the AFL-CIO just before the attempt on his life. One year later he returned to address the same group:

I know you all understand how happy I am to be back—standing before you today. If it's all the same to you, though, when I finish speaking, I think I'll slip out the back door this time.

6 ☆ "Remember the Code of the West"

L et it be said of this generation of Americans that when we passed on the torch of freedom to the new generation, it was burning just as brightly as when it was handed to us.

Mr. Reagan, speaking to veterans, relating a true story about the bridge on the River Kwai:

Near its banks is a cemetery, the final resting place for those who died building that bridge and that railway. Many of the grave markers are inscribed with nothing more than a name and a service number.

Yet now and then there's a small monument, built by a father or a mother or a widow who trekked halfway around the world searching for a marker with a very special service number.

On one of these monuments, erected by a woman named Irene, are the following words: "To the world, you were only one; but to me, you were all the world."

I feel a sacred trust to America's soldiers and citizens alike— I feel a sacred trust to protect their lives and their liberty.

Mr. Reagan, at the marine barracks, for a change-of-command ceremony:

I issue the new orders from your commander in chief. On behalf of all Americans, I want a message sent to every member of the corps, to every place where the words *Semper Fidelis* is a way of life.

General, tell it to the marines, whether in ceremonial white or leatherneck blue, whether in dress greens or combat camouflage, whether they serve in the air, on land, or at sea. Tell them that their countrymen are grateful. Tell them that we're proud of our proudest.

Mr. Reagan welcomed Hispanic leaders to the White House with the words, "Mi casa es su casa," and then recalled how he first heard the phrase when he was governor of California:

We had experienced heavy rains, and so I visited an area in Santa Barbara where there had been great mud slides. I was there to see what the damage was and how we could be of help to forestall this from happening in the future.

An elderly gentleman of Mexican descent motioned to me

and invited me to come into his home. And there we stood in the wreckage of what had been his living room, both of us knee-deep in muddy water.

And with the greatest dignity he said to me, *"Mi casa es su casa."*

☆

Mr. Reagan, speaking to those in government who would raise taxes:

We survived a Great Depression that toppled governments. We came back from Pearl Harbor to win the greatest military victory in world history.

Today's living Americans have fought harder, paid a higher price for freedom, and done more to advance the dignity of man than any people who ever lived.

We have in my lifetime gone from the horse and buggy to putting men on the moon and bringing them safely home.

Now, don't tell us that we can't be trusted with a greater share of our own earnings.

☆

A group of young Americans was touring Latvia a few years ago. They were given an opportunity to visit with a local artist.

This painter, careful with her words because she was speaking through a government interpreter, suggested that the artist fared better under communism because the system demanded quality before an artist's work could be shown, thus preventing an undeveloped artist from ruining his or her reputation.

This painter, for example, said she had worked hard and was soon to be permitted a showing in Moscow. She pulled out some examples of her work, and, as is so often the case with socialist realism, her work lacked a certain personality and feeling.

Before the young Americans could leave, however, this artist insisted that they see examples of her earlier work, before her skills had matured enough for a showing in Moscow. She removed from her closet some photographs of her earlier paintings, paintings that were alive with expression, reflecting warmth and vitality.

She had given those young Americans a message without ever having to say a negative word about artistic freedom under totalitarianism.

☆

If we're free to dare (and we are), if we're free to give (and we are), then we're free to shape the future and have within our grasp all that we dream the future will be.

☆

Mr. Reagan's Christmas dedication:
Some celebrate Christmas as the birthday of a great and good philosopher and teacher.

Others of us believe in the divinity of the child born in Bethlehem, that He was and is the promised Prince of Peace.

Yes, we've questioned why He who could perform miracles chose to come among us as a helpless babe, but maybe that was his first miracle, his first great lesson, that we should learn to care for one another.

Tonight, in millions of American homes, the glow of the Christmas tree is a reflection of the love that Jesus taught us.

Like the shepherds and wise men of that first Christmas, we Americans have always tried to follow a higher light, a star, if you will.

At the lonely camp fire vigils along the frontier, in the darkest days of the Great Depression, through war and peace, the twin beacons of faith and freedom have brightened the American sky.

At times our footsteps may have faltered, but trusting in God's help, we've never lost our way.

☆

Mr. Reagan's strong Irish heritage can be felt in all that he says and does. This speech, before the Irish Historical Society, tells a lot about the Irish in the President:

There is the legend in Ireland of the happy colleen of Ballisodare who lived gaily among the wee people, the tiny people, for seven years, and then when she came home discovered that she had no toes. She had danced them off.

I feel happy enough with you here tonight, when I get home I'm going to count mine.

Nancy is sorry that she couldn't be here, and so am I. She sends her warm regards and her regrets. Unfortunately, on the last trip into town she picked up the bug.

Now, I'm happy to say that's not the situation for me—like the two sons of Ireland who were in the pub one evening, and one asked the other about his wife.

He said, "Oh, she's terribly sick. She's terribly ill." And the other one says, "Oh, I'm sorry to hear that. Is there any danger?" "Oh, no," he said. "She's too weak to be dangerous anymore."

Anyway, a writer for the Irish press who was based in Washington stated about me that I have only recently developed a pride in my Irish heritage, and that up until now I have had an apathy about it. Well, let me correct the record. That is not so. I have been troubled until fairly recently about a lack of knowledge about my father's history.

My father was orphaned at age six. He knew very little about his family history. And so I grew up knowing nothing more beyond him than an old photograph, a single photo that he had of his mother and father, and no knowledge of that family history.

But somehow, a funny thing happened to me on the way to Washington. . . .

When I changed my line of work a while ago, it seemed that I became something of an interest to people in Ireland, who very kindly began to fill me in. And I have learned that my great-grandfather took off from the village of Ballyporeen in County Tipperary to come to America. And that isn't the limit to all that I have learned.

Some years ago, when I was just beginning in Hollywood in the motion-picture business, I had been sentenced for the few years I'd been there to do movies that the studio didn't want good, it wanted them Thursday.

And then came that opportunity that every actor asks for and hopes for, and that was a picture that was going to be made of the biography of the late Knute Rockne, the great immortal coach of Notre Dame. Pat O'Brien was to play Rockne.

There was a part in there that from my own experience as a sports announcer I had long dreamed of, the part of George Gipp.

Generously, Pat O'Brien, who was then a star at the studio, held out his hand to an aspiring actor, and I played the Gip. My playing the Gip opened the door to stardom and a better kind of picture.

I've been asked at times, "What's it like to see yourself in the old movies, the reruns on TV?" It's like looking at a son you never knew you had.

But I found out that Pat O'Brien's family also came from Ballyporeen. And I've been filled in on much more since then. A historian has informed me that our family was one of the four tribes of Tara, and that from the year 200 until about 900 A.D., they defended the only pass through the Slieve Bloom Mountains. They held it for all those centuries and adopted the motto: The Hills Forever.

And that, too, is strange, because for many months now I've been saying much the same thing, only in the singular: The Hill Forever. Capitol Hill, that is.

I do remember my father telling me once when I was a boy, and with great pride he said to me, "The Irish are the only people in the country, in America, that built the jails and then filled them."

I was a little perturbed even then, at that tender age, because at the sound of pride in his voice and from the way I'd been raised, I couldn't quite understand why that was something to be proud of.

It wasn't until much later that I learned that he was referring to the fact that the overwhelming majority of men wearing the blue of the police department in America were of Irish descent.

I was on a mission to Europe for our government, and we wound up in Ireland.

On the last day I was taken to Cashel Rock. We looked with great interest at those ancient tombstones and the inscriptions.

And then we came to one on which the inscription said, "Remember me as you pass by, for as you are, so once was I. But as I am, you too will be, so be content to follow me."

That was too much for the Irish wit and humor of someone who came after, because underneath was scratched, "To follow you I am content; I wish I knew which way you went."

☆

Mr. Reagan, in November 1981, hosted a ribbon-cutting ceremony to welcome the press corps to the newly remodeled White House press briefing room.

The briefing room was formerly a swimming pool, up until the time President Nixon ordered it covered to accommodate the expanding press corps.

In attendance was James Brady, to whom the briefing room was dedicated.

Mr. Reagan welcomed the press corps back and, reminding them that the room was over a swimming pool, said there was no truth to the rumor that the floor was hinged and could be sprung like a trap.

Mr. Brady chuckled and said that yes, it was hinged.

Mr. Reagan went on to say that a new feature had been installed—the place was now wired for sound; just by pressing a button he could get helicopter noise to drown out questions.

James Brady

When Mr. Reagan cut the ribbon, he quipped that he had been practicing all morning on Mr. Meese's tie.

Mr. Brady then asked Nancy Reagan if he was still her Y and H.

Taken back, Mr. Reagan facetiously said the husband is always the last to know.

And Mrs. Reagan finally gave in, telling the amused reporters and her husband that Jim Brady was still her young and handsome.

It was a day for the White House staff, joined by James Brady and the reporters, to enjoy a laugh and a smile or two.

☆

I hear all those voices every day that say we can't succeed. Well, if we only put our heart and courage to the test, I say we cannot fail.

To those who are fainthearted and unsure, I have this message: If you're afraid of the future, then get out of the way; stand aside. The people of this country are ready to move again.

☆

Fostering the faith and character of our people is one of the great trusts of responsible leadership.

I deeply believe that if those in government offer a good example, and if the people preserve the freedom which is their birthright as Americans, no one need fear the future.

Unfortunately, in the last two decades we've experienced an onslaught of such twisted logic that if Alice were visiting America, she might think she never left Wonderland.

☆

Mr. Reagan was asked what was the low point in his presidency:

If you don't mind my saying it, maybe the low point came when I got out of the car and walked into the emergency room of George Washington Hospital—and was told I'd been shot.

I thought that the Secret Service man who piled in on top of me in the car had maybe broken a rib. I knew I hurt, but I didn't know I'd been hit. And I had a bullet just about one inch from my heart.

☆

When that great philosopher and commentator de Tocqueville came to America from France, he took a long look at our country and wrote, "If anyone asks me what I think the chief cause of the extraordinary prosperity and growing power of this nation is due to, I should answer, it is due to the superiority of the women."

Well, his words are still true today, only I would add, especially our Republican women.

Standing up for America also means standing up for the God who has so blessed this land.

If we could just keep remembering that Moses brought down from the mountain the Ten Commandments, not ten suggestions—and if those of us who live for the Lord could remember that He wants us to love our Lord and our neighbor, then there's no limit to the problems we could solve or the mountains we could climb together as a mighty force for good.

The United States remains the last, best hope for a mankind plagued by tyranny and deprivation.

America is no stronger than its people—and that means you and me.

Well, I believe in you, and I believe that if we work together, then one day we will say, "We fought the good fight. We finished the race. We kept faith." And to our children and our children's children we can say, "We did all that could be done in the brief time that was given us here on Earth."

☆

El Salvador has continued to strive toward an orderly and democratic society.

The government promised free elections, and after months of campaigning by a variety of candidates, the suffering people of El Salvador were offered a chance to vote, to choose the kind of government they wanted.

It was then that the so-called freedom fighters in the hills were exposed for what they really are—a small minority who want power for themselves and their backers, not democracy for the people. The guerrillas threatened death to anyone who voted. They destroyed hundreds of buses and trucks to keep the people from getting to the polling places. Their slogan was brutal: "Vote today, die tonight."

On election day, an unprecedented 80 percent of the electorate braved ambush and gunfire and trudged for miles, many of them, to vote for freedom.

One woman standing in line to vote was heard to say, "You can kill me, you can kill my family, but you can't kill us all."

We can never turn our backs on that.

☆

Mr. Reagan, on the second anniversary of his administration:
My, how time flies when you're having fun. A lot can happen in two years. Just looking around this room, I can see the signs of change everywhere. Judging from this group, I seem to have given more gray hairs than I got during the last two years. I guess you can chalk that up to the luck of the Irish. . . .

To all of you loyal members of our team, please let me express my deepest appreciation for what you're doing.

Sometimes when I think of how much you do and how little recognition you get, I find myself reminded of a story about Orville and Wilbur Wright.

They had tried repeatedly to get off the ground with their new flying contraption. They had one disappointment after another.

And then finally, on one December day there at Kitty Hawk, Orville did what no man had ever done before.

It had to be the greatest news scoop in history. They wired their sister Katherine, "We have actually flown 120 feet. We'll be home for Christmas."

When she received the wire, she ran all the way to the local newspaper office and handed the wire to the city editor of her local paper. He looked at the wire and said, "Well, isn't it nice! They're going to be home for Christmas."

Anyway, we were sent here to move America forward again by putting people back in charge of their own country; to promote growth by placing limits on the size and power of government; to give individuals the opportunities to reach for their dreams; to strengthen the institutions of family, school, church, and community; to make the United States a stronger leader for peace, freedom, and progress abroad; and, through it all, to renew our faith in God who has blessed our land.

☆

Mr. Reagan was briefing members of the media on defense spending. Both the President and the reporters were all wrapped up in the briefing.

Unexpectedly, Mrs. Reagan peered into the briefing room in full view of the reporters but out of her husband's vision.

The President continued, emphasizing that in the 1960s defense spending was 10 percent of the gross national product, it was 8 percent in the 1970s, by 1979 it had come down to 5 percent, and his administration was holding it to no more than 7 percent.

Some of the reporters had begun to giggle because they could see the First Lady waiting impatiently for her husband to stop talking.

Mr. Reagan continued on, eager to make his point, but he could not understand why the reporters were laughing.

Finally, the First Lady burst in with a birthday cake all lit up for the President—it was, after all, two days before his birthday.

The briefing was forgotten as everybody sang "Happy Birthday" to the President and told jokes:

REPORTER: What did you wish?

PRESIDENT: You can't tell what you wish because then it won't come true.

FIRST LADY: That's right. And you have to take the first piece.

PRESIDENT: I have to take the first piece? I'll spoil my lunch.

FIRST LADY: You have to take the first piece.

PRESIDENT: I'd have cut it smaller if I'd known that.

REPORTER: Mrs. Reagan, have you any resolutions you want him to make on his birthday? Anything you want him to do differently?

FIRST LADY: I think he's doing just fine.

SAM DONALDSON, ABC NEWS: Well, maybe this would be a

good time for you to tell him if you think he should run again.

FIRST LADY: Oh, no.

DONALDSON: You're not getting too old to run again, are you, sir?

FIRST LADY: How would you like a piece of cake, Sam?

PRESIDENT: As a matter of fact, Sam, since she cut that one smaller, here, take mine and I'll trade.

FIRST LADY: No, no, no. That's bad luck.

PRESIDENT: I have learned not to argue with her superstitions.

CHRIS WALLACE, NBC NEWS: Do you feel up to six more years, Mr. President?

FIRST LADY: How about a piece of cake for you?

LARRY SPEAKES, PRESS SECRETARY: Yes, give Sam and Chris a piece so they'll quit talking and start eating.

REPORTERS: But you understand, we don't sell out for a piece of cake. No deals.

PRESIDENT: Oh, you've sold out for less.

REPORTERS: Do you have any observations on your birthday, Mr. President? I mean any thoughts about the future?

PRESIDENT: It's just the thirty-first anniversary of my thirty-ninth birthday. I'm enjoying every one of them. And I think that it's fine when you consider the alternative.

I confess, I was not always as attentive as I might have been during my classroom days. I seem to remember my parents being told, "Young Ron is trying, very trying."

But I also remember the attitudes and actions of my parents and teachers. Sometimes stern, sometimes gentle, always they strived with quiet courage to teach us responsibility, discipline, honesty, tolerance, kindness, and love.

Mr. Reagan was speaking at a reception honoring the Outstanding Handicapped Federal Employees of the Year:

Ronald Reagan (second row, left) with schoolmates

You may face limitations, but not one of you lacks the courage, the will, or the heart to do what others say cannot be done.

There's a young lady with us today who has demonstrated that so well. Jennifer Boatman has spina bifida, a serious malformation of the spine. Well, Jennifer's handicap didn't stop her from saving the life of a five-year-old boy.

When Jennifer saw young Joshua Mikesell tumbling through a whitewater stretch of the North Umpqua River in southwestern Oregon, she didn't hesitate one second. She jumped into the swift mountain stream, swam to the boy, and pulled him to the riverbank.

Joshua's father called it a miracle. It's also the story of the courage and the capability of America's disabled. And for all of us it's the ultimate expression of love. Greater love hath no man than to lay down his life for a friend.

We must hold out the exciting prospect of an orderly, compassionate, pluralistic society, an archipelago of prospering communities and divergent institutions, a place where a free and energetic people can work out their own destiny under God.

☆

A few years ago someone figured out that if you could condense the entire history of life on Earth into a motion picture that would run for twenty-four hours a day, 365 days, this idea we call the United States wouldn't appear on the screen until three and one-half seconds before midnight on December 31.

And in those three and one-half seconds not only would a new concept of society come into being, a golden hope for all mankind, but more than half the economic activity in world history would take place on this continent.

Free to express their genius, individual Americans—men and women—in three and one-half seconds would perform such miracles of invention, construction, and production as the world had never seen.

☆

Although the voters believe by overwhelming margins that waste and fraud in government are among its most serious problems, I notice that whenever I talk about it, the eyes of many of my friends in the media glaze over, and they stop taking notes.

Well, I've figured out how to interest the press corps. We're going to call a secret meeting of our inspectors general, tape-record the proceedings, stamp the transcripts Top Secret, stuff them in a diplomatic pouch, and accidentally leave them on Lou Grant's doorstep.

A leaked story will always be used.

☆

Mr. Reagan was asked by a reporter about his thoughts on the television industry and current programming:

Well, this is just my personal opinion. I'm not very happy about the industry I used to be in—I liked it better when the actors kept their clothes on. It isn't just morals, it's lousy theater. The oldest rule of theater is that nothing you can do on the stage or screen is as good as the audience's imagination. . . .

I think motion pictures made single beds popular because one of the rules was that you could not show two people, even married, in a bed together.

I played a picture one day in which Doris Day was my wife. We were supposed to be in bed together, and the audience will never know that they never saw us together. They saw me looking out the window awake in the night; they saw me look over my shoulder and then get out of bed, put on a robe, and start around the foot of the bed. And then they saw Doris lying there in the other side of the bed.

Well, I'd like to see those days back.

The West won't contain communism, it will transcend communism.

I accept without question the words of George Washington: "To be prepared for war is one of the most effectual means of preserving the peace."

Now, in spite of some things you may have heard, he didn't tell me that personally.

Don't tell us that we can't cope with our problems. Don't tell us that America's best days are behind her. The world's hope is America's future. America's future is in your dreams. Make them come true.

Like death and taxes, the doom criers will always be with us—and they'll always be wrong about America.

☆

It was one of those nights in California in the storm season, and down at Newport Beach the homes along the beach were being destroyed, washed away by the high tides and the waves that were breaking against them. The TV stations were down there covering the story, and it was about two in the morning.

I was still watching TV, and you could see the volunteers working through the night to sandbag the homes and try to save them.

And at two in the morning, it can get awfully cold there—California is the only place in the world where you can fall asleep under a rosebush in full bloom and freeze to death. And this one lad was still in his swimming trunks. He was wet and cold and tired, but he was still lugging those sandbags.

Well, one of the TV commentators caught him and got him in front of the camera. Did he live in one of those houses? No, he said, he didn't live there at the beach. And finally the question came, well, why, why was he doing this? And his answer was so poignant. He said, "Well, I guess it's the first time any of us ever felt we were needed."

Well young man, you are needed. With men and women like you, there is no limit to what we can do.

☆

I've always believed that this blessed land was set apart in a special way, that some divine plan placed this great continent here between the oceans to be found by people from every corner of the Earth who had a special love for freedom and the courage to uproot themselves, leave homeland and friends to come to a strange land. And in coming here they have created something new in all the history of mankind.

☆

Our moment has arrived. We stand together shoulder to shoulder in the thickest of the fight. If we carry the day and turn the tide, we can hope that as long as men speak of freedom and those who protected it, they will remember us and will say, "Here were the brave, and here is their place of honor."

☆

Mr. Reagan, illustrating his dream of eliminating the risk of nuclear war:

The Soviets and we have differences in governmental structure and philosophy. But we have common interests that have to do with everyday life. Just suppose that an Ivan and an Anya could find themselves, oh, say, in a waiting room or sharing a shelter from a storm with a Jim and Sally, and there was no language barrier to keep them from getting acquainted. Would they then debate the differences between their respective governments? Or would they find themselves comparing notes about their children and what each other did for a living?

Before they parted company, they probably would have touched on ambitions and hobbies and what they wanted for their children and problems of making ends meet. And as they went their separate ways, maybe Anya would be saying to Ivan, "Wasn't she nice? She also teaches music." Or Jim would be telling Sally what Ivan did or didn't like about his boss. They might even have decided they were all going to get together for dinner some evening soon.

Above all, they would have proven that people don't make wars.

7 ☆ "Sincerely Yours, America"

A young sailor wrote to tell me that he was writing for his 180 crewmates on a submarine, and he said, "We just want you to know how good it feels once again to be Americans. . . . We may not be the biggest navy, but we're the best."

☆

I received a letter from a little girl in the fifth grade. It was very well written and correctly punctuated and not a word misspelled.

But with the letter came $187 that this fifth grade class had raised and sent in to be applied to the national debt.

When I was in fifth grade, I'm not sure I knew what the national debt was. Of course, when I was in fifth grade, we didn't have one.

Shortly after I got here, I received a letter from an eleven-year-old girl telling me in some detail about the matters I would have to deal with. I must say, I was greatly impressed.

I don't think at eleven years I could have written someone and explained the international affairs and economic situation the president is faced with.

But she told me and offered some solid suggestions on what to do, and then wound up with a postscript. She said, "Now get over to the Oval Office and go to work."

In Illinois the other day, I met a young lady named Stacy.

Now don't jump to conclusions, Stacy is only in the sixth grade.

And Stacy had just won a statewide essay contest, and she was pretty imaginative because her essay was a letter to our country.

It started, "Dear America, I just thought I should write you a letter to let you know how great I think you are."

I'm not going to read the entire essay, but she closed her letter to America saying, "It really doesn't matter whether we're black or white, atheist or Christian, your doors of opportunity are always open. So knock, knock, America, here I come."

I received a letter from our ambassador to Luxembourg one

day, and he said that he had been up to the East German frontier to visit the Second Armored Cavalry Regiment.

He said a young trooper followed him over to his helicopter and asked him if he thought he could get a message to the president.

The ambassador allowed as how he could, so the young fellow said to him, "Will you tell the president that we're proud to be here, and we ain't scared o' nothin'."

☆

I received a letter which I wish could be delivered to all Americans. It happens to be from one of our young sailors on a carrier out in the Pacific. They came upon a sinking boat of Vietnamese refugees, and they brought them to shore.

Now, this letter is from the boy to his mother and father telling about that day. And he said, "It was awful hard to talk when you had a lump between your chin and your belly button."

The way he ended was so articulate and so inspiring: "I hope one thing will always be true of our country. I hope that we will always be the place where anyone from any place in the world who is in need and in trouble can come, and we'll find room for them no matter how many they may be."

☆

I received a message from the father of a marine in Lebanon. He told me, "In a world where we speak of human rights, there is a sad lack of acceptance of responsibility for the privilege of living in this country.

"My son has chosen the acceptance of responsibility for the privilege of living in this country. Certainly in this country one does not inherently have rights unless the responsibility for those rights is accepted."

☆

I have received some letters from the families of some of those who were on that Korean airliner that the Soviets so brutally destroyed.

One was from a mother whose twenty-eight-year-old daughter was on the plane. She had lost her husband the year before through a terrible illness. Her daughter had two children. So now the grandmother had to tell those two children that their mother was dead.

And she told me how the little six-year-old boy turned without a word, and then a short while later came back and handed her a drawing he had made of a little boy crying, and said, "That's how I feel."

I sometimes think that if it would do any good, I'd like to send a lot of those letters to Mr. Andropov.

A grade school class in Somerville, Massachusetts, recently wrote me to say, "We studied about countries and found out that each country in our world is beautiful and that we need each other. People may look a little different, but we're still people who need the same things."

They said, "We want peace. We want to take care of one another. We want to be able to get along with one another. We want to be able to share. We want freedom and justice. We want to be friends. We want no wars. We want to be able to talk to one another. We want to be able to travel around the world without fear."

And they asked, "Do you think that we can have these things one day?"

Well, I do. I really do. Simple wishes may seem far from fulfillment. But we can achieve them. We must never stop trying.

☆

A private citizen in Louisiana asked the government for help in developing his property. He received back a letter that said, "We have observed that you have not traced the title

105

prior to 1803. Before final approval, it will be necessary that the title be traced previous to that year." Well, the citizen's answer was eloquent.

"Gentlemen," he wrote, "I am unaware that any educated man failed to know that Louisiana was purchased from France in 1803. The title of the land was acquired by France by right of conquest from Spain. The land came into the possession of Spain in 1492 by right of discovery by an Italian sailor, Christopher Columbus. The good Queen Isabella took the precaution of receiving the blessing of the Pope. . . . The Pope is emissary of the Son of God, who made the world.

"Therefore, I believe that it is safe to assume that He also made that part of the United States called Louisiana. And I hope to hell you're satisfied."

One Ohio businessman writes us about his personal frustration with burdensome regulations. He cites an item from the Toledo area Small Business Association bulletin.

"It is reported to us," the item read, "that the Lord's Prayer contains 57 words. Lincoln's Gettysburg Address has 266 words. The Ten Commandments are presented in just 297 words, and the Declaration of Independence has only 300 words."

And then it goes on to say, "An Agriculture Department order setting the price of cabbage has 26,911 words."

Another letter was addressed: "To the aide opening this letter. I didn't vote for you, I voted for Ronald Reagan, and I want him to read this letter."

And I read it!

The lady said, "I'm a farm wife, sixty years old, not too well educated, but it doesn't take too smart a person to see and feel what's going on. I know you have a lot of things to do and decide, but have you ever stopped and thought about the farmer?

106

"Stop and think: Can a farmer pay seventy-five to one hundred thousand dollars for a combine? Can he pay the price for fertilizer, seed, you name it, and sell corn, wheat, and soybeans for the price they are today?"

She said, "Just because farmers aren't out carrying strike signs or tearing something up doesn't mean they're not hurting. What farmers want is a fair price so they can pay their bills and feed their families."

She was only wrong about one thing, that maybe I hadn't time to think about farmers. The farmers of America are very much on my mind.

Patricia Morgan of Florida writes that she sees unity among us again, the kind of unity we had during World War II—we Americans, all pulling together. That's what America is. That is our power. Patricia Morgan, I couldn't agree more. American power is reasserting itself again.

I received a call from a union worker, before the 1981 Solidarity Day march in Washington, to tell me that he not only wasn't going to go but to show me a copy of the letter he had sent to the head of his union explaining why the union shouldn't go and why they should be in support of what we're trying to do. The courage of that man was exciting and thrilling.

And then came a letter from a sixteen-year-old boy who said, "From what's going on there, I'm sure that you're going to save the country for kids like me."

A lady down in New Orleans wrote to tell me that she was black, she told me her age—I won't reveal it here, but she was very elderly—and then she told me, "Thanks for destroying the war on poverty. Maybe now we at last can get back to growing our own muscles and taking care of ourselves the way we should."

Received a letter from a retiree the other day. It contained his check for civil service retirement, a full month's retirement endorsed over to the Treasury Department because he said he just wanted to help us get the job done.

☆

A letter came in from a lady in Illinois who told me that she was one of three CETA employees at the time when we were changing that program. She said, "I just want you to know that there is only work enough for one of us. We don't need three. As we came to the end of the last fiscal year, there was money left over."

She continued, "I was ordered to go out and buy new office furniture because we couldn't have any money left over or the grant money might be reduced for the coming year. So here I sit at my great new executive desk with nothing to do."

Well, I thought that was too much, so I called in some of my staff, read them the letter, and said she deserves better than she's got. And you know something? She is now employed in a $25,000-a-year job out in the private sector and happy with her work.

She says it sure beats daytime TV.

☆

The *Des Moines Register and Tribune* invited grade school children to write letters to the paper advising the president on his job.

One eleven-year-old boy wrote, "When you get there, don't look to the past, look to the future. You won't have time to look to the past. Make up your mind that when you leave there you will be older and tired, and there will be a few more gray hairs on your wise old head."

And then he said, "Just get to the office, go to work, and

108

be happy that you're only president, you don't have to be God."

Out of the mouths of babes.

☆

Mr. Reagan, speaking to supporters a few weeks after the American liberation of the island of Grenada from Communist aggressors:

I received a copy of a story written by one of our air force pilots for the *Armed Forces Journal*. He recounted as how he noticed that every news story about the Grenada rescue mission contained a line that Grenada produces more nutmeg than any other place in the world. He decided that was a code, and he was going to break the code—and he did:

"Number one, Grenada produces more nutmeg than any place in the world. Number two, the Soviets and the Cubans are trying to take Grenada. Number three, you can't make good eggnog without nutmeg. Number four, you can't have Christmas without eggnog. Number five, the Soviets and the Cubans are trying to steal Christmas. And number six, we stopped them."

☆

This letter had to be translated from braille. A GI who had lost his sight in World War II in Germany wrote, in braille, to tell me that if cutting his pension would help get this country back on its feet, he'd like to have me cut his pension.

Well, we're not going to cut his pension. But we are going to get this country back on its feet.